*The Closer
You Look*

THE
GREATER
THE
BOOK BIBLE PROOFS

GEORGE S. SYME CHARLOTTE U. SYME

ACCENT BOOKS
Denver, Colorado
WITHDRAWN

MEMBER OF
EVANGELICAL CHRISTIAN
PUBLISHERS ASSOCIATION

First introduced in 1968 as The Scriptures Cannot Be Broken, this work has been revised by the authors and updated to include the latest archaelogical findings and other external evidences to demonstrate that the Bible is indeed the eternal Word of God.

Accent Publications
12100 W. Sixth Avenue
P.O. Box 15337
Denver, Colorado 80215

Library of Congress Catalog Card Number: 76-8731
ISBN 0-916406-20-2

Contents

Preface

In all this topsy-turvy, mixed-up, thoroughly confused world, we know of one thing that is completely consistent and reasonable — the Holy Bible. We make this statement categorically, and we make it from the starting assumption that the Bible is the Word of God and is therefore perfectly trustworthy and absolutely without error.

We have not written this book to prove our statement; with or without external evidence, we cling to that on the testimony of the One who said, "Thy word is truth" (John 17:17). What we have attempted to do is to demonstrate for the benefit of those who have been taught otherwise that our faith has a far more reasonable basis than do the objections of those who have sought to undermine it. They also accept by faith the assumptions on which their objections are based.

Over many years of teaching experiences we have been frequently shocked by the attitude of those who do not want to know the criticisms and problems that have been raised against the Bible. Said one businessman: "Why should I listen to the criticisms of those who tear down the Bible? They would never keep me from believing it." Or a Bible college student: "Why should I spend time reading and analyzing what these critics write against the trustworthiness of the Bible? Why don't you just tell what to believe?" And a Sunday School teacher: "I don't have to understand the viewpoint of the Bible critics. They are all the devil's emissaries."

Yet the Sunday School teacher taught children who were beginning to notice that the science they learned in school appeared to contradict some things they had been taught at home and church. The Bible school student planned to enter the ministry. He could expect members of his congregation to turn to him when they heard arguments and criticisms they could not answer. Furthermore, he would be in frequent contact with other ministers, many of whom would take for granted the theological positions he did not want to "waste time" reading.

The Christian businessman had teenage children who had listened to teachers ridicule the Bible as an unscholarly book. They had been assured that "all scholars agreed" it contained many errors of fact. (An interesting sidelight on the Biblical expertise of some high school teachers is the observation that when one yearbook quoted Ecclesiastes 3:2 but attributed it to the Beatles, no one caught the error.)

This businessman also subscribed to several popular magazines and took particular interest in the articles which frequently appeared on Biblical and other religious subjects. Invariably these articles assumed the position that the religion of the Bible "evolved over many centuries to a high level of ethical monotheism that was not known before the time of the prophets." Frequently there were references he did not understand — "Second Isaiah," "the priestly writer," "the J document."

Jesus said that the children of this world are wiser than the children of light (Luke 16:8). We have not grown much wiser since He said it. A good football coach spends many hours studying slow-motion movies of his opponent's games. Every military commander gathers as much intelligence as possible about his enemy's weapons and tactics. An alert manufacturer wants to know the strengths and weaknesses of his competitor's products. But the children of light say, "Why should we study the attacks made on the Bible?" — the very root and foundation on which our faith rests.

Such an attitude borders very closely on anti-intellectualism. It goes along with those who say, "Education breeds doubt and we had better avoid it." It is an attitude which really shows as little faith as does the opposite one that says, "We must accept the findings and results of modern scholarship."

Such an avoidance of problems feeds the subconscious fear that the foundation will reveal cracks if the light of knowledge shines on it. Jesus said, "The scripture cannot be broken" (John 10:35). Since He speaks truth, the only thing light can do is to reveal more clearly the firmness of the foundation.

The purpose of this book is to shine the light of human knowledge on the Scripture at the very points where human knowledge has claimed to uncover its weaknesses and thereby to reveal there is nothing there, after all, to cause us to stumble.

These chapters are not reasons why we believe the Bible is true. We believe it because we believe the One in whose care we have placed our lives and our eternal destinies. Rather, these studies are evidences of the reasonableness of our faith and hope. Peter admonished us to give a reason to all who ask (I Peter 3:15). Among those most likely to ask are our alert young people who begin very early to question the discrepancies between what they are taught in school and hear from friends, and what they learn at home and in church. If we are afraid of what human scholarship may disclose, they will sense it and scorn our faith. Can we afford to fail them by refusing to be prepared with reasons? Can we afford to let fear fester in the dark closets of our faith? Do we trust the One who said through Isaiah, "The word of our God shall stand for ever" (Isaiah 40:8)?

This work has not been addressed to the scholar, but to the Christian layman who desires to "be ready always to give an answer to every man that asketh you a reason of the hope that is in you" (I Peter 3:15).

There may be some readers, however, who do not

enjoy this hope. To them we say we have "written, that ye might believe that Jesus is the Christ, the Son of God; and that believing ye might have life through his name" (John 20:31).

We therefore submit this work to you, as Peter concludes, "with meekness and fear."

George S. Syme
Charlotte U. Syme

Souderton, Pa.

1

THE UNITY OF THE WORD
Evidence from the Unity of Scripture

A young man who all his life was taught that the Bible is God's Word, which he must believe and live, went away to college. He sat under professors who sought to "educate" him out of his faith. They "proved" that the Bible was not written by the men who claimed to write it or at the times when it was supposed to have been written. Some pointed to "contradictions" and "errors" which they assured him were matters on which "all scholars were agreed." Others told him it contained spiritual rather than historic or scientific truth or that it represented "the noblest thoughts of man groping after the eternal."

As the student lost faith in the Book he began to copy worldly companions. In time he cast aside sobriety, purity and honor. If the Bible was not God's Word in truth, he needed no longer to be "different" or bound by its stern, wholesome way of life.

SCRIPTURE IS ONE BOOK

Must this be the fate of any young Christian exposed to secular education? Is the Scripture really only a mixed collection of truth and error through which we may browse to find some nuggets of spiritual truth? Look at your Bible. It contains sixty-six books, written by nearly forty people, who lived at various times over a period of fifteen hundred years. There were shepherds, fishermen and politicians among its writers. There were also scholars, noblemen and royalty. They wrote of many subjects and used many literary forms — history, biography, poetry, drama, letters.

Seeing all this diversity, the superficial student jumps to mistaken conclusions. Says one: "The authors who wrote the Bible . . . were human beings like ourselves and as prone to make mistakes . . . Many of their own erroneous ideas naturally got mixed in with the truth that came to them from God."[1] Another declares: "The Bible contains much history, some of it faintly embedded in age-old myths, folk tales, battle songs, camp fire recitals and the like."[2]

But to those who really know the Book it is not many but one. Writers were carefully chosen, and the Spirit of God so controlled them in the recording of God's message, as to give us His Word with divine and infallible authority. From beginning to end it is consistent; it has one message and one subject. The Apostle Peter, in his letter to the believers dispersed throughout Anatolia (Asia Minor), tells us what that one subject is. You will find it in I Peter 1:9-12. The coming of Christ — His work and His glory, and the salvation which He would make possible — is the one subject of the Scripture. II Peter 1:21 tells us, "For the prophecy came not in old time by the will of man: but holy men of God spake as they were moved by the Holy Ghost."

How did Peter know? He had learned it from the lips of the Saviour Himself. Walking with Him day after day, listening to His disputes with the Pharisees, he heard it many times. "I am come to . . . fulfill [the law and the prophets]," Jesus said (Matthew 5:17). On another occasion He commanded, "Search the scriptures . . . they are they which testify of me" (John 5:39).

Probably the most thrilling declaration of this truth that was ever made came on the day of the resurrection (read Luke 24). Two followers of the Nazarene, mourning His death, were walking sorrowfully toward home when they were joined by One who later revealed Himself as their risen Lord. He disapproved of their grief because it revealed how little they had understood their Scriptures. Then, "beginning at Moses and all the prophets, he expounded unto them in all the scriptures the things concerning himself" (Luke 24:27).

This must have been the most thrilling Bible class that has ever been conducted; and just a little while later it was repeated for the benefit of Peter and the other apostles. As they sat in the upper room discussing the strange events and reports of the day, the Lord Himself appeared among them and reminded them of all He had previously taught. "These are the words which I spake unto you, while I was yet with you, that all things must be fulfilled, which were written in the law of Moses, and in the prophets, and in the psalms, concerning me. Then opened he their understanding, that they might understand the scriptures" (Luke 24:44,45).

This statement reveals that the Hebrew Bible Jesus knew contained the same three basic divisions that are found in it today: 1) The *Torah* (Law of Moses, or first five books); 2) The *Nebiim* (or Prophets, which comprise Joshua, Judges, Samuel and Kings, known as the former prophets; and Isaiah, Jeremiah, Ezekiel and the twelve minor prophets, known as the later prophets); 3) The *Kethubim* (the Writings, which begin with Psalms, contain all the books not in the other two, and end with Chronicles). In ancient times it was customary to name a book by its first word or title. Thus by referring to Psalms in Luke 24:44, Jesus was including all the *Kethubim*.

On two earlier occasions He had said, "From the blood

of Abel until the blood of Zechariah" (Luke 11:51; compare, Matthew 23:35). Certainly Zechariah was not the last to shed his blood for the faith. The only logical explanation is that here again Jesus referred to the Old Testament Scriptures in the order in which they still exist in the Hebrew text. Abel was slain at the beginning of the first book, and Zechariah's death is recorded in II Chronicles, the last book in their arrangement.

Some have argued that this three-part division of the Old Testament Scripture was not accepted until the Council of Jewish rabbis at Jamnia about A.D. 90. These references, however, clearly reveal that our Lord expounded the Scriptures in the same form in which they have been handed down to us. And He said they all concerned Himself.

Jesus Christ is the subject of all the Bible. It is all one great story — including the romance of salvation. Why do you need a Saviour? How was a Saviour to be given? What plans and preparations did God make to provide us one? Were there hindrances or obstacles? Did the Saviour ever come? Did He fulfill His mission? Does He have present plans for men? Future ones? Will they be fulfilled?

All this is told. The need, the promise, the fulfillment, and the victory are all detailed for our understanding. Surely this is one Book with one subject. And those forty or more authors — how did they ever agree? Many of them without any contact with one another, separated by both many miles and many centuries, how did they tell the story so accurately? Peter answered this question for us too. "Holy men of God spake as they were moved by the Holy Ghost" (II Peter 1:21). God spoke through these men. He impressed upon them His truth, and through them He spoke to us. They themselves did not always understand what they wrote, as Peter again informs us (I Peter 1:10,11), but faithfully they spoke as they were taught.

This is not meant to imply that the prophets and apostles were mere tape recorders on which the divine Spirit dictated His message. Each one reveals much of his own character, personality, and background in his writing. He presents God's revelation in the framework of his own experience and of the times and culture in which he moved. Just as sunlight shining through a lovely stained glass window falls on the floor of the church in a multi-colored splash of light revealing many of the parts that make it up, so the light of God filtering through the personalities and culture of the writers revealed various facets of His truth, which altogether made up the whole of His revelation, but all were under the direction of the Spirit of God.

Thus, despite differences of style and language, all the writers spoke the Word of God, becoming the windows of His mind and heart. We can say with assurance as did Peter: "We have also a more sure word of prophecy; whereunto ye do well that ye take heed, as unto a light that shineth in a dark place" (II Peter 1:19). The Scripture is a sure word because there is *one divine Author*, God the Holy Spirit, who directed the work of its *many writers*.

IT STANDS OR FALLS AS A UNIT

A high school senior came face to face with a basic life decision. His teacher had challenged him to defend his faith. He thought it through carefully. Could he accept a materialistic philosophy to explain life, or should he turn to the Bible — God's explanation? It became clear to him that either he must accept the whole Scripture or none of it, for who was qualified to say that one verse was God's Word and another was not? He determined then and there to choose God's way of faith in the Scriptures. Somehow, even though he was not at that time acquainted with II Timothy 3:16, he had grasped the import of its meaning: "All scripture is given by inspiration of God, and is profitable for doctrine, for reproof, for correction, for instruction in righteousness."

The young man mentioned earlier, whose college career ended so tragically, was in one way consistent. If the Bible was not true in what it had to say about history or science or any other subject on which it could be checked, why should anyone rely upon it when it spoke of God and Heaven and sin and salvation? As Jesus once said to a learned man who came by night to speak to Him, "If I have told you earthly things, and ye believe not, how shall ye believe, if I tell you of heavenly things?" (John 3:12).

We cannot treat the Bible like a tray of appetizers, picking and choosing among its contents. Either it is God's Word and is all true, or it is not worthy of the study and devotion that we lavish upon it. The Neo-orthodox[3] take the opposite viewpoint.

Neo-orthodoxy says, "The Bible becomes the Word of God to you whenever it speaks God's message to you." This means that inspiration is a purely subjective matter. If it inspires you, then that part of it which does so becomes an inspired Word. On such a basis "Amazing Grace," or even one of Shakespeare's plays may be as equally inspired as the Twenty-third Psalm. According to such a theory, the first two chapters of Luke may be inspired for you, but not for your neighbor who refuses to accept the reality of the virgin birth. If this theory is what _inspiration_ means, then God has not spoken and man is under no obligation to listen. One's own fallible judgment becomes the criterion for inspiration and for deciding what to obey.

A woman whose pastor taught these theories, showed him a Bible mutilated by missing pages, gaping holes, and passages pasted over with blank paper. "Whatever you have taught me not to trust I have removed," she said. "Now I have so little left that I don't feel I can trust it either — not for this life or eternity. Where can I turn?"

If revelation is revelation only when it is acknowledged, where is authority? If God has spoken, He has spoken regardless of whether man listens.

Paul writing to Timothy, his young colleague, impresses on him the truth that all Scripture has been breathed by God and all of it is profitable for the maturing of the Christian man (II Timothy 3:16,17). Timothy had known the Scripture all of his life, having learned the Old Testament from his mother and grandmother long before he met Paul. Perhaps he felt he knew it well enough. But Paul urges him to continue in the things he had learned and proceeds to give him the reason. Paul says that all Scripture is profitable. As Christians then, we do not approach a given passage in order to see whether or not it is God's Word because of the way it inspires or fails to inspire us, as Neo-orthodox scholars would like us to think. If we do not sense that God is speaking to us through it, we should ask ourselves why. Our approach is to study it further to find His message, or search our hearts to see what sin has closed our channel of understanding. It is not for us to judge the Word of God, but for the Word to judge us.

Our Lord gave plenary (full, complete) inspiration to His Word by means of the Holy Spirit in order that we might trust the New Testament. These apostles were made eyewitnesses of the resurrection in order that they might have all the necessary evidence to believe the claims of the One about whom they were commanded to witness. Three of them had the privilege of seeing Him transfigured into His glorified appearance and Peter refers to that experience as being for him one of the outstanding evidences of the truth of the deity of Christ. Yet, he adds, "We have also a more sure word of prophecy" (more sure than the awesome experience of the Transfiguration!) and that more sure word is the Holy Scripture (II Peter 1:19-21).

The Christian faith is built on historic facts. The fact

that the first human pair defied God and plunged their descendants into helpless alienation is a basic foundation which supports all that follows. If the fall of Adam is a myth, our Christian theology is meaningless. There is no explanation then for the world's evil, or for man's misery and inclination to do wrong. The human condition becomes the bad joke of a whim of fate.

God promised our first parents a Redeemer, and to prepare man to receive Him, He chose out a nation. That nation, Israel, had a history, a spot of earth on which to dwell, and interrelations with other nations. They left their traces, discernible to historians and archaeologists. And much of what God has told us concerning them is duplicated in the records of their neighbors and enemies.

He instructed His people how to recognize His prophets. If their predictions came true, He had spoken. If not, they were false and need not be heeded (Deuteronomy 18:21-22). Many false prophets did attempt to confuse Israel. They fought Elijah on Mount Carmel (I Kings 18:18-24); they opposed Micaiah before Jehoshaphat (I Kings 22:6-14); they defied Jeremiah before the fall of Jerusalem (Jeremiah 23:15-16; 28:1-17). We remember them now only to their humiliation. God's true spokesmen, whose words Israel carefully preserved, were increasingly vindicated as their long-range prophecies came true.

At a definite time and place Israel produced its most illustrious Son, who claimed to be both God and man. He lived, and His life and deeds were widely reported. He died violently at the hands of His enemies, but He had already forewarned His followers that He chose it that way for the purpose His death would fulfill. After three days He rose from the dead and imbued His followers with a power and faith that changed history. Destroy any one of these facts and the Christian church has no meaning. We cannot otherwise explain its formation and its continued existence in the face of all the efforts made to annihilate it. It behooves us who have staked our lives — and our eternal destinies — on the Truth revealed in this Book to be sure of the firmness of the foundation on which our faith rests.

After the crucifixion, one of the apostles thought he saw all that he had lived for blown down like the straw house of the first little pig. He refused to entertain further false hope. Read about Thomas in John 20:24-31 and notice his stubbornness. I absolutely will not believe without evidence, was his determination. And the Lord graciously gave him the evidence he asked for. He knows that we are weak in faith, and from the beginning He has provided evidence to corroborate His spokesmen. Even today, through the continuing researches of men — many of whom do not even acknowledge Him — He provides evidence to an age of doubt for the Truth of His Word.

This is what the study of Christian evidences is all about. We shall see how every department of human knowledge — history, geography, anthropology, science, language, and psychology — contributes something to substantiating the Word of God. We will study a few of these contributions in detail. But by no means can everything in the Bible be so tested. Our present knowledge has barely penetrated the fringes of God's wisdom and His works. But — and this is even more important — neither can we prove anything in the Word to be false. God says that "without faith it is impossible to please him" (Hebrews 11:6). That does not mean He has required our faith to be unreasonable. He has given us the marks to recognize His prophets so as to trust His Word.

But, someone says, why should we bother about what the ungodly have said against the Book, and why should we refute them? Is it not of greater value simply to believe it and to study it? Why not tell our children, "This is truth," and keep from them the doubt-producing teaching of others?

The boy whose story is told at the beginning of the chapter is the answer. He was taught to believe the Book. He was not told that it had detractors and that their arguments were puny. He was not told that the faith taught him was built on fact and reasonableness, that it had nothing to fear from advancing frontiers of knowledge and discovery. Thus, when the storm came, his life building collapsed on its sandy foundation.

Furthermore, had he been one of today's youth, he would have met such doubts long before college. It floods today's education even as early as fourth grade. And some Sunday School literature teaches it! We cannot keep their minds hedged in.

Peter, still writing to the scattered believers of Asia Minor whose faith he had so highly praised, advised them to "be ready always to give an answer to every man that asked you a reason of the hope that is in you" (I Peter 3:15).

We have hope and we have faith. Let us for ourselves and for our children study to have a reason for them. We are not setting out to "prove" the Bible but to attest its inspiration and authority at those points where it touches the realm of human knowledge. As we progress through this study of Christian Evidences our hearts should be blessed with a deeper assurance that we hold in our hands God's message to mankind.

2

THOSE "MYTHOLOGICAL" PATRIARCHS
Some Biographical Evidence

A history textbook in current use says: "The epic incidents in which the patriarchs passed through experiences that gave them a stature above that of ordinary mortals — such as Jacob's wrestling with an angel, Isaac's survival of his father's ritual sacrifice, and Abraham's speaking with God — were interwoven with folk tales common to many peoples and were combined with elements from other mythological systems "[4]

This comment is not unusual. Our children grow up learning one thing at home and in Sunday School but something altogether different in school. We lead them to believe that Adam and Eve, Enoch and Noah, Nimrod and Terah were living, breathing, historical characters who were actually residents of our planet and influenced their contemporaries. Educators, however, tell them that these personalities never really existed except in the fancies of Bible writers. Our generation needs to know whether any evidence exists for the reality of the patriarchs who lived before Moses.

THEIR BACKGROUND WAS REAL

That patriarchs were nomads who traveled extensively and we can still identify the places that were associated with them. A *National Geographic*[5] article on Abraham speaks of priests first recording the story about one thousand years after the events supposedly occurred (an admission of its Wellhausen orientation) and about which "they had neither recollection nor record." Yet the author admits the record is remarkably accurate concerning its geography and its social history. Writers of this persuasion like to call the accuracy of Genesis remarkable, whereas those who accept an inspired Bible take it for granted.

Had Genesis been produced as a purely human writing as late as the eighth century B.C., the author would surely have placed Abraham in towns known to him and not mentioned places long since forgotten. Yet consistently we see the patriarchs stopping at places known by archaeological excavations to have flourished in their time, but afterward buried and forgotten until modern times. Never once are they described as visiting a place that has been demonstrated not to have existed in their day.

In order to appreciate the evidence for the historical fact of the Genesis account, it is necessary for us to understand what the "higher critics" teach and on what they base their conclusions. When in the middle of the nineteenth century Darwin's theory of evolution captured the imagination of scholars, they began to see it not only as a theory of biological development but as a basic philosophy underlying every subject — including theology.

According to the Darwinian-inspired view, man, as he became less apelike, developed nobler concepts of God. First, he put spirits in every object. Then the important spirits of the universe became gods. Then each man or tribe or political division picked a personal protecting god, and the Hebrews decided theirs was the only one. Only as late as Amos and Isaiah did God's character become moral and loving. Once scholars assumed all this, the next step was to redate the writing of the Bible so that any passage which seemed to have a "primitive" concept of God was called early and any which taught a highly moral concept was called late.

A German scholar named Wellhausen (who lived until 1918) first popularized this theory. It is usually called by his name or the "Documentary Hypothesis" because he taught that the Old Testament was a more or less haphazard collection of documents put together by an unknown editor who gave them a flowing unity by adding his own comments. This theory denies that Moses wrote the first five books and attributes them to the four chief writers of the Old Testament. We should know something about these views because they appear so often in popular writing.

J, the first of these writers (who liked to call God *Jehovah*), was supposed to live in Judah about the ninth century B.C., at the time of Elijah. E (who preferred the name *Elohim* for God) wrote a century later in Ephraim, or the northern kingdom, about the time of the prophet Amos. D (or the Deuteronomist) is placed in the seventh century B.C., at the time of Josiah and Jeremiah and gets credit not only for writing Deuteronomy but for compiling Joshua, Judges, Samuel and Kings. The keystone of this theory is the assumption that the book found in the Temple (II Kings 22:8) was only the book of Deuteronomy, which was thus published for the first time Lastly, in the days of Ezra (fifth to fourth century) there was P, a priest who wanted to defend the idea that the Jews needed a religion of ritual as opposed to a religion of social justice supported by the prophets. P may have been a committee! He or they are responsible for everything extolling ritual and ceremony (such as Leviticus) and also for the genealogies (family tree records), since holding the office of priest depended on being a descendant of Aaron.[6]

It was further assumed that the first written material was the national documents of the kings of Israel. Later they wrote down and preserved the legends of their early history and rise as a nation. Still later, as their outlook widened, they added "mythologies" of human beginnings with which they were familiar (meaning Genesis 1-11).

One reason this confused theory found such easy acceptance when it was proposed was the complete lack at that time of historical records of early Mesopotamia (the region of the earliest human civilization, the area from which Abraham originated) and Canaan. Even the great Hittite Empire had vanished from history, being known only from occasional Old Testament references. Thus it seemed fantastic to non-believers to look at Genesis and the times of the patriarchs as sober history.

While Old Testament scholars sat in their studies analyzing the text and producing a patched-up Pentateuch (the first five books of the Old Testament) with successive verses attributed to different authors, archaeologists were introducing scientific methods. They were discovering the value of comparative stratigraphy[7] and pottery in dating the remains of ancient literature of Egypt and Babylonia. Hundreds of thousands of tablets were uncovered, so many that most remain to this day unread in museum basements — providing more recent scholars with a new type of excavation.

After World War I Mesopotamia swarmed anew with archaeologists who unearthed new treasures. At Mari and Nuzi many tablets from patriarchal times were uncovered which are of great interest to us because of the light they shed on the customs of those times.

Mari was a powerful city located on the Euphrates River in Syria near the Iraqi border. Nuzi is located in Iraq, east of the Tigris River, near modern Kirkuk. It is southeast of the ancient site of Nineveh, and its modern name is Yorghan Tepe.

Abraham's possession of camels has long been held in question by reputable archaeologists who maintained they were not really domesticated and used as beasts of burdens before the period of the Midianite raids in the times of the Judges. Parrot's excavation of Mari turned up enough new evidence for him to say, "As far as we are concerned, and supporting ourself by archaeological documentation, it is our opinion that camels were a part of the patriarchal corral and that consequently the mention of camels in bibilical texts belongs to reality and not to the imagination of some editor who is caught in an anachronism."[8]

The documents from Mari and Nuzi consist of business records, legal papers, and personal correspondence. They reveal the flourishing civilization of the long lost Hurrians (Biblical Horites) who inhabited the world through which Abraham, Isaac, and Jacob moved, especially the city of Haran. Abraham considered Haran his "country" where his "kindred" lived (Genesis 24:4). These excavated documents show that the social customs and manners of the Hurrians were the same as those practiced by Abraham and his family.

Among the Nuzi tablets are documents which show that a man without an heir may adopt one (especially a houseborn servant) with the understanding that should he later have a natural heir, that one will take precedence over the adopted one. This custom is referred to by Abraham in Genesis 15:2-4.

Again, marriage contracts from Nuzi specify that if a wife proves childless it is her duty to provide her husband with a foreign slave for the purpose of giving him an heir. The wife, not the slave, has authority over such a child, and if she later bears a son, the slave-child, though older, may be set aside. Abraham and Sarah did not invent the solution to their problem in making Hagar a concubine (Genesis 16). Their lapse of faith caused them to revert to prevailing customs with the attitude, "Why not? Everybody does it."

With the newly discovered history of the patriarchal era (2000-1700 B.C.) thus spread before the world, the Wellhausen Hypothesis should have retreated to a quiet resting place. Unfortunately, like Darwin's theory which spawned it, it appeals too strongly to the natural man who does not want to believe or become subject to God's Word. Yet even the scholars who accept this theory must admit that the book of Genesis coincides exactly with what we know about the history and customs of that era. E.A. Speiser, a scholar who writes for the popular press and who accepts Wellhausen, says, "The patriarchal narrative in Genesis — the story of Abraham, Isaac and Jacob — has a legendary flavor. But many details of the story are now confirmed and elucidated by outside sources, particularly archaeological data relating to the very region of Mesopotamia which the patriarchs called their home. This area was dominated by the Hurrians, whom the Bible calls Horites. The discovery of vast numbers of clay tablets recording Hurrian laws and customs has provided substantial evidence that Abraham and his family followed the local social practices."[9]

E.A. Speiser, Old Testament scholar and Anchor Bible translator of Genesis, who accepts the Wellhausen hypothesis, makes this significant statement: "Since by such examples, the background of the Abraham story has emerged as authentic, one is prompted to ask whether the foreground, too, may not be factual on the whole And the foreground in this instance is the dramatic content of the story."[10]

THEY WERE REAL PEOPLE

We divide Christian Evidences into two parts which we call internal and external. Internal refers to evidence which we find within the Scripture itself; external refers to evidence from history, science, linguistics, archaeology, or any other place which relates to the Scripture and helps to demonstrate its authenticity. The places and customs and times in which the patriarchs lived we have discussed in relation to external evidence.

However, it is one thing to prove a historic background real and quite another to prove the individual real. A writer of historical novels may give an authentic background for the period he writes about and yet use fictional characters. How do we know that this was not the case with the Genesis record?

Remember that Abraham and his family were nomads and did not leave buildings and monuments to attest their presence as settled peoples do. Most of their wealth was in the form of livestock and portable items. Although Abraham was promised the whole land of Canaan for an inheritance, the only piece of land he ever actually owned was a burial plot. The traditional site of these family graves, plus that of Rachel near Bethlehem, are our chief external evidences for the reality of the patriarchs. Visitors to modern Hebron may enter the mosque which is built over the cave where several of the patriarchs are buried, but permission to go below into the cave is rarely granted by the Moslem owners.

England's Disraeli, asked by a skeptic to prove the Bible in a word, answered, "Jew." The existence of the Jew is both an external and an internal evidence of the historicity of their founding father, Abraham. The existence throughout the Bible of carefully kept genealogical records by which every Jew could sustain his claim of descent from Abraham and from one of Jacob's twelve sons is internal evidence. Our Lord's claim to be the fulfillment of the Abrahamic promise is attested by His genealogy. Unless He were Abraham's seed, He would not fulfill the Scripture.

Genealogical records were largely destroyed when Jerusalem was destroyed by the Roman armies of A.D. 70. But even now many Jews keep as careful genealogies as possible. Those named Cohen or Kahn are especially likely to maintain careful records because these names suggest descent from the priestly families.

The Arabs, who claim Abrahamic descent through Ishmael, also keep careful genealogies. W.F. Albright, the noted Palestinian archaeologist, says he has sat around Arab campfires and listened as they recited long genealogies and histories going back many generations. One minor change from the set form brings quick correction.

Our Lord knew Abraham was a real person and referred to him as such (Matthew 8:11; John 8:33-39, 52-58). One of His arguments for the resurrection of the dead is based on the historicity of Abraham, Issac, and Jacob (Matthew 22:32). Dare we doubt what He stated? Even His enemies, much as they longed to catch Him in error, did not dispute Him here. Neither did they dispute Stephen when he stood on trial and reminded the Jews of their history (Acts 7:2-9).

One of the internal evidences to their historicity is the fact that the patriarchs were so human. They had many faults, and these faults are not glossed over as is so often the case with legendary heroes. Jacob, for example, had enough faith and spiritual insight to value the inheritance of the Abrahamic Covenant as Esau, the materialist, did not. Yet Jacob did not have enough faith or moral uprightness either to get it honestly or to trust God to give it to him as He promised in Genesis 25:21-23.

We, in fact, are inclined to be more guilty of glossing over their faults than were the Bible writers. For example, we learn from some unearthed tablets that a custom of patriarchal times permitted men of prestige and importance to confer special status on their wives by adopting them as sisters. Thus Speiser and others suggest that Abraham had quite likely done this, pointedly honoring Sarah by so introducing her to Pharaoh and Abimelech (Genesis 12:13-20; 20:2-18). Speiser suggests that the eighth-century writer who supposedly (according to Wellhausen) wrote down the story did not know of the long-forgotten custom and so assumed that Abraham must have had a deceitful motive for his actions.

One Christian man reading this explanation expressed pleasure at learning that Abraham was not a liar after all. He was not at all aware of the dangers inherent in his attitude, but was led astray by seeing Abraham's character enhanced. Had the article said Abraham never existed, or that the incident never occurred, he would have been indignant. He did not see that this whitewash of a hero equally undermined God's inspired revelation. If this is God's Word, then the God who knows the inmost heart (I Samuel 16:7) has laid bare Abraham's basic motive (even though he might have hushed his own conscience by reference to such a legal technicality — Jeremiah 17:9). To accept Speiser's tempting explanation on this point is to accept the Documentary Hypothesis and to deny the plenary inspiration of the Scripture.

God Himself wanted us to know that His heroes were sinners, even as you and I. As He used them in spite of their weaknesses, so He can use us. The patriarchs' stories are given to encourage us. Had they been painted as perfect, they could not have been "a cloud of witnesses" to us but a discouragement. We would say, "Of course such as they pleased God." But we know them to be disobedient, deceitful, polygamous. They were sinful men with a great and merciful God. If they could please Him long before the cross by basing their hopes on His promises, cannot we, who have seen the love of God manifested at Calvary and the promises fulfilled, rest our faith and destiny on Him, even to the place of laying aside the sins which so easily beset us?

Will we not, in the same way, prefer to rest our faith on the certainties of God's Word regardless of what others may say about it? We have everything to lose and nothing to gain by substituting for such assurances the assumptions based on man's limited knowledge and his rejection of the knowledge of God.

COULD MOSES WRITE?
Evidence from Archaeology

A few years ago a major denomination published a Sunday School lesson for young teens that expressed a classic doubt — that the Pentateuch (the first five books of the Bible) must have been written many years after Moses' death, for probably he could not write. Here is the quotation: "Folks used to think that Moses wrote all these books, but the best Bible scholars now tell us this is not so . . . As a matter of fact, the books of the Pentateuch, in their present form, were written many years after Moses' death . . . We don't know for sure that he wrote anything, or that he knew how to write!"[11]

The attractive and up-to-date literature of many denominations is now slanted to the viewpoints of so-called "assured results of modern scholarship." If your children are spared this in Sunday School, it reaches them through their world cultures textbooks and articles on Biblical subjects in popular magazines. We need to take a look at the flimsy foundations of these conclusions.

GOD PREPARES A MAN

We are not going to "prove" Moses wrote the

Pentateuch. We accept it on the internal evidence of God's Word. The Bible itself (our internal evidence) does not allow us any other view but that Moses could and did write. Before the nineteenth century his authorship was never seriously questioned. The Pentateuch itself makes numerous claims of Mosaic authorship (Exodus 17:14; 24:4; 34:27,28; Numbers 33:2; Deuteronomy 31:9,22). Other Old Testament writers recognized Mosaic authorship (Joshua 1:7,8; 23:6; I Kings 2:3; II Chronicles 23:18; Ezra 3:2; Daniel 9:11,13; Malachi 4:4). Even our Lord accepted Mosaic authorship (Mark 10:3; Luke 16:31; 24:27,44; John 5:45-47). Other New Testament writers confirm Mosaic authorship (Acts 3:22; Romans 10:5; I Corinthians 9:9; Revelation 15:3).

In spite of all this evidence, the Wellhausen Hypothesis established itself on two foundation crutches: 1) that writing was not known in Palestine at the early date when Moses lived; and 2) that so detailed a law code was too advanced for so primitive a time in man's history. Because this hypothesis has slowly filtered from university to seminary to pulpit and, in our generation, to the man on the street and even the child in school and Sunday School, it is important to realize that these crutches have splintered under the weight of historical and archaeological advance.

As far back as 1904, Sir William Ramsey recognized that the argument that writing was not common could no longer be used against Mosaic authorship.[12] Yet critics continued to raise it. In 1941, Sir Frederick Kenyon, former curator of manuscripts at the British Museum had this to say: "It is not long since it was commonly maintained that the books of the Pentateuch could not be based on contemporary records, much less be attributable to Moses himself, because writing was not known at that time. Eminent scholars in the last quarter of the nineteenth century, such as Wellhausen and Graf, held that writing was not known in Palestine before the time of the kings. Here archaeology has come to our assistance most decisively."[13]

The critics forgot that even if Palestine had not known writing in 1500 B.C., the Egyptians admittedly did, and "Moses was learned in all the wisdom of the Egyptians" (Acts 7:29). "All the wisdom of the Egyptians" was a considerable body of knowledge. They were expert architects as shown by the intricate pyramids which were built a thousand years before Moses. Because of their obsession with mummification they acquired an advanced knowledge of anatomy and other medical information and some chemistry. They were acquainted with astronomy and invented the solar calendar. They were expert mathematicians, using geometry long before Euclid toyed with it.

Most important to us, it is quite possible that Moses could use four different scripts, three of them learned in Egypt. The Hieroglyphic picture-writing incised on the buildings and tombs of Egypt was by his time used by scribes in a simpler cursive form called Hieratic. In addition, extensive foreign correspondence was carried on in the Babylonian cuneiform (wedge-shaped).

Furthermore, as a prince of the royal court, Moses would have studied law and government and learned to participate in settling legal disputes brought to the court. How ironic! Without that inhuman decree of Pharaoh (Exodus 1:16,22), Moses would not have had the opportunity for a court education. God's purposes will not be thwarted. He uses the wrath of men both to praise His name and to further His plans (Psalm 76:10).

However, the impetuous young prince needed the polish of a forty-year graduate course. In the desert he learned wilderness geography by the practical method of leading flocks of sheep around it. Here he probably became acquainted with a fourth script — the alphabetic writing invented by the Canaanites (know to history as the Phoenicians). For — unknown to nineteenth-century scholars — Palestine did have writing. It is called the Sinaitic alphabet because the earliest known samples were discovered in 1904-5 by Sir Flinders Petrie in the Sinai peninsula.

Even though Petrie could not read the script, he did recognize its importance and made this statement: "It finally disproves the hypothesis that the Israelites, who came through this region into Egypt and passed back again, could not have used writing. Here we have common Syrian labourers possessing a script which other Semitic peoples of this region must be credited with knowing."[14]   Despite the fact that such discoveries continued to appear in site after site in Palestine, doubt of Moses' ability to write continued to appear forty years later and reliance upon the Wellhausen documentary hypothesis continues to appear in current publications.

Later, in 1929, discoveries near Ugarit (modern Ras Shamra) showed that even the cumbersome cuneiform had at an early date been simplified to an alphabet, and a few years ago a tablet listing the alphabet in its modern Hebrew arrangement was found.

Ugarit was an ancient Canaanite seaport in northern Syria opposite Cyprus. A library discovered there not only tells us much about the religion and culture of the Canaanites, but also demonstrates that many things which the late nineteenth-century and early twentieth-century critics thought were evidences of late authorship of the Pentateuch were actually common in this city destroyed before 1200 B.C. Not only did Moses write, it is quite possible he did his writing in an alphabetic script that is the ancestor of our own.

GOD USES HIS SERVANT

Forty years is a long time. Eventually Moses was all but forgotten at court. Most of his enemies and friends, even Pharaoh's daughter, may have died. Surely when he returned he found many changes. But God had preserved his older brother and sister, Aaron and Miriam, for the work He had for them.

God had three tasks for Moses. One was the preservation of the records of His earliest dealings with man and choice of a people through whom to send His Messiah. The ability to write was indispensable for this. Then his immediate work was to rescue the seed of Abraham from their Egyptian bondage. And third, Moses had to make them a nation and provide them with the instruments of government. The basic instruments of government are a compact or covenant (for Americans the Constitution) and a body of law by which to uphold and enforce it. It was at this law that critical theologians aimed the second of their attacks. Detailed bodies of law, they thought, did not appear until much later.

Those who doubted Moses' ability to write also doubted his ability to produce an elaborate law code. They knowingly explained that the Mosaic codes were too advanced for the era in which he lived. Such an assumption overlooked two facts: 1) Brought up at court, Moses would be experienced in legal matters and settling disputes; and 2) other peoples had laws equally detailed.

The critics did not know about Hammurabi, who was a king of Babylonia several centuries before Moses. He was an empire builder and the king who destroyed Mari, the city whose excavation shed so much light on Abraham's time. His capital city, Babylon, was a center of learning, art, and literature. Ancient epics, legends of the gods and early history were collected. These collections were written in two languages — Akkadian and Sumerian.

Hammurabi was one of history's earliest lawgivers, writing down a detailed code of law for the regulation of affairs among his subjects. History knew nothing of this until 1901 when a copy of his laws was uncovered by archaeologists at Susa, an ancient capital of Persia (Shushan in Esther and Nehemiah). Marauders had carried it away on one of their raids against Babylon. We have since discovered more early codes.

The natural man does not want to believe the Bible because it exposes his sin and demands he answer to God for it. Sooner or later the true nature of his criticisms and arguments show through. Faced with the evidence of detailed laws older than Moses, he turned about-face and said, "O well. Moses (or the P writer) copied Hammurabi."

Of course the two lawgivers take up the same subjects. The crimes men commit against one another have been similar in all times and places. Crimes against private property, against the person, and against the marriage contracts have needed to be judged by all rulers. Hammurabi set standards and settled disputes to keep order in Babylonia.

Moses discussed these crimes too, but he also dealt with attitudes of hate, of covetousness, of envy. These are inner disciplines — the root of active crime — but against which no earthly judge can presume to legislate and enforce conformity. Only God can touch these, and God claimed to speak through Moses.

At the head of the slab of Hammurabi's Code is a picture of the king standing before the sun god, Shamash. "See," say the critics, "Hammurabi, too, claimed to receive his law code from his god." Does he? No such suggestion appears in any part of the code, and there is no record that Hammurabi made such a claim. The picture itself is not decisive. Hammurabi could just as easily be presenting his laws to the god or seeking Shamash's approval of them.

There are many basic differences between the Mosaic legislation and that of Hammurabi and the Assyrian, Hittite, and others that have come down to us.

1. There is a different *emphasis.* Moses is spiritual; Hammurabi is civil. Moses' commands are the commands of God to men; he takes no credit or authority himself. Hammurabi, on the other hand, takes all the credit. He is

the divinely appointed king, and it is he who presumes to curse anyone who defies his laws. Hammurabi's laws deal only with individual offenses. He does not presume to deal with the root of wrongdoing — with sin. In Hammurabi's code there is nothing comparable to "Thou shalt not covet." This is an attitude not subject to mere legal control.

2. There is a different *theism*. The Mosaic law is clear and concise: "Hear O Israel the Lord our God is one Lord" (Deuteronomy 6:4). Opposed to this clear monotheism stands the gross polytheism of Hammurabi's prologue and epilogue.

3. There are different *ethical and moral concepts*. Hammurabi is not interested in regulating ethics and morals. He quotes no proverbs. He is interested merely in regulating those cases where the individual citizen turns to the state for redress of a grievance against another. His desire is to maintain order in his kingdom to prevent the anarchy which follows when men exact their own vengeance.

On the other hand, the God of Moses claims vengeance as His prerogative (Deuteronomy 32:35). He expects, "Thou shalt love the Lord thy God with all thine heart, and with all thy soul, and with all the might" (Deuteronomy 6:5). All who scorn moral and ethical standards are in defiance of God. The wronged are commanded to love — "Thou shalt not avenge, nor bear any grudge against the children of thy people, but thou shalt love thy neighbor as thyself: I am the Lord" (Leviticus 19:18). Morality has nothing to do with the Code of Hammurabi; it has everything to do with the Law of Moses.

4. There is a different *application*. Hammurabi's legislation obviously applied to those under his temporal sway. The Mosaic Code, based upon divine sway, obtains universal application. There is nothing in the codes of the ancient Near East to compare with the universality of the Decalogue.

It is encouraging to know that the critics do not have a crutch to stand on. That knowledge will help us to help young or weak Christians and those with honest questions who are seeking a faith. But it is more important to keep in mind that long before archaeologists had found ancient alphabets and law codes, there were Christians who believed God rather than the critics. And long, long before Wellhausen, Jesus affirmed that Moses wrote the Pentateuch (John 5:45-47). If we cannot believe the Son of God, then who or what can we believe?

4

THE JUDGE OF ALL THE EARTH
More Evidence from Archaeology

Robert Ingersoll, the Victorian infidel who once nursed hopes of running for the United States presidency, criticized the Bible in 1881 in these words (among thousands of others): "In all civilized countries it is now passionately asserted that slavery is a crime; that war of conquest is murder . . . that nothing is more infamous than the slaughter of decrepit men, of helpless mothers, and of prattling babes . . . Nations entertaining this view are now regarded as savage, and with the exception . . . of a few tribes . . . no human beings are found degraded enough to agree on these subjects with Jehovah."[15] Ingersoll died before twentieth-century events could refute his optimism, and many of his scientific arguments were answered even by his contemporaries, yet his lectures are even today favored hunting grounds for quotations to justify infidelity and his attitudes are echoed by pacifists and opponents of capital punishment.

THE JUDGMENT OF THE HEATHEN

Doubters have long flung this same challenge in the face of those who accept all the Scripture as being the revelation of one God. Somehow they feel it justifies them for rejecting its claims on their lives. How shall we reply? On the one hand we read the commandment, "Thou shalt not kill" (Deuteronomy 5:17). On the other hand we have God saying to Israel, ". . . thou shalt save alive nothing that breatheth: But thou shalt utterly destroy them" (Deuteronomy 20:16,17). Is this a contradiction? In the first instance, the verse should be translated, "Thou shalt not murder." The second refers to warfare; and killing in warfare is not murder.

Infidelity lacks creative originality, disinterring the same old lies generation after generation. Whenever someone undertakes to undermine your faith in the Scripture, or at least to justify himself for not accepting it, he will sooner or later tell you that the God of the Old Testament is not the loving Father that Jesus talked about. Almost certainly he will ask, "What about the slaughter of the Canaanites?" Well, what about the slaughter of Canaanites? Here admittedly was a case of total war involving civilian populations as well as armies; and furthermore, God sanctioned it. It was part of His plan for history. Does it reveal an arbitrary and capricious god such as the Canaanites themselves worshiped, or is it a true revelation of the God and Father of our Lord Jesus Christ?

Genesis 15 records the covenant God made with Abram, promising that his seed would be as the stars of Heaven. He also promised him the land "from the river of Egypt unto the great river, the river Euphrates" (Genesis 15:18). However, these promises would not receive immediate fulfillment, for God assured: ". . . thy seed shall be a stranger in a land that is not theirs, and shall serve them; and they shall afflict them four hundred years" (verse 13). He explained to Abram the reason for the four hundred years of servitude in a strange land: "for the iniquity of the Amorites is not yet full" (Genesis 15:16). Who were these iniquitous Amorites and others whom God would later command Israel to destroy? In Abram's time the term "Amorites" was used loosely to refer to the people of Syria-Palestine.

What kind of people were these Canaanites that such utter devastation should have descended upon them? The complete list of the peoples of the land recurs several times in Scripture as "the Hittites, and the Girgashites, and the Amorites, and the Canaanites, and the Perizzites, and the Hivites, and the Jebusites" (Deuteronomy 7:1). They had one of the most advanced cultures of the ancient world. Situated at the crossroads of the great trade routes on a land bridge between Asia and Africa, they were history's middleman, controlling its commerce. They were also the great seafarers among the ancients. You will remember them from history as the Phoenicians, for that is the name by which the Greeks called them. The coastline abounded in a shellfish that was the ancient world's principle source of purple dye. Therefore the Greeks called it the Purple (Phoenician) Coast and the people Phoenicians (the purple people). The demand for their dye, carved ivory (elephants still roamed Syria) and other products, brought them into trade contacts with numerous cultures and they became wealthy. Their lives were enriched by luxuries from all the known world.

Great cities flourished, made wealthy by the commercial activities. In the second millennium B.C., there were Sidon, Byblos and Ugarit on the coast. The first millennium B.C. saw the rise of Tyre to dominance. In the Hellenistic Age, Antioch was founded and became the most important Syrian trading center of New Testament times.

Such metropolitan centers — gathering places for traders from all over the world — would disseminate much more than their alphabet and their dyestuffs. Their beliefs, activities, and morals would inevitably influence faraway hinterlands. When God looked down upon them, He saw their corrupt morals offsetting by far their material contributions. In Leviticus 18:3, He warns His people: "After the doings of the land of Egypt, wherein ye dwelt, shall ye not do: and after the doings of the land of Canaan, whither I bring you, shall ye not do; neither shall ye walk in their ordinances." Then follows such a list of grossly disgusting sins that they are rarely read in public.

From this and other Old Testament passages, persons of faith have always realized that the Canaanites were steeped in gross immorality. The Old Testament charges that they frequently offered up their children as living burnt offerings to their bloodthirsty gods. But it remained for modern archaeology to turn up countless naked female figures, the so-called "astarte" plaques, and the remains of their burnt sacrifices in order to bring home to us in vivid horror the reality of these Old Testament allegations. The Israelites were to have nothing to do with either the Canaanites' gods or their sensual worship rituals.

Certainly they were far more advanced culturally than the nomadic Hebrews who conquered them. Comparison of the archaeological remains of their great walled cities (Deuteronomy 1:28; 6:10) with the rude villages of the first generation of Israelites to follow them, bears this out. They were, in addition, stronger and more powerful than the people of Israel. The Old Testament tells us that they already had the seeds of destruction within themselves (Genesis 15:16; Leviticus 18:25-28; Deuteronomy 9:4,5). Like a great tree eaten of termites, their inner decay made them ripe for judgment.

"The land is defiled," God said (Leviticus 18:25); "therefore I do visit the iniquity thereof upon it." His judgment did not fall overnight as it had upon Sodom and Gomorrah. The rest of Canaan should have taken that judgment as a warning and should have repented in light of it. But they didn't, and God waited until their iniquity was "full." It was time "the land itself vomiteth out her inhabitants" (Deuteronomy 18:25b).

Genesis 15 foretells the fate of the people of Canaan more than four hundred years before Joshua actually invaded the land. Yet they continued to buy and sell, to grow rich, to build beautiful cities, to heap iniquity upon iniquity, unaware that they were inviting the greater damnation.

Leviticus 18, which records their sins in dreary detail and does not make pleasant reading, should have convinced any man with even a small portion of faith that their destruction was not a matter of injustice or a whim with Jehovah, nor a mere playing of favorites for the benefit of His chosen people. Some of the ancient historians also described the corruption of the Canaanites and the depraved rituals by which they worshiped their fertility gods and goddesses.

But it remained for a Syrian farmer's plowhorse stumbling into a hole to unearth for us the first clues which brought to light the daily life and activities of the ancient Canaanites. If you have never read the story of the Ugaritic excavations at Ras Shamra, you will profit by doing so. This and later Canaanite excavations have confirmed the Bible and the Greek historians (who had also been doubted and accused of exaggeration). Theirs was a sex-centered religion, their gods were in the likeness of the worst of men, and many of their orgies were performed as acts of worship to their gods. Professional prostitutes, both men and women, were permanently attached to the temples.

It has often been asked why there should be inserted in the center of a catalog of sexual sins, such as Leviticus 18, the prohibition against burning children as sacrifices to Molech (verse 21). The answer becomes clear when we see that the unifying factor of all these sins is the fact that all were performed as ritual acts of worship to the Canaanite gods.

Remember that the Canaanites dwelt at the ancient

world's crossroads and their teachings and manner of living were spread by the caravaneers. How long should a God of love be expected to allow such corruption to spread to the hinterlands to infect all of humanity?

Certainly the Canaanites had been warned. The awful destruction of the Canaanite cities of Sodom and Gomorrah (Genesis 19) was surely meant as an example to bring them to repentance. Abraham, Isaac, and Jacob, with their testimony to the nature of the true God, had lived three generations among them.

Genesis 38, which often on casual reading seems to be an unnecessary intrusion into the story of Joseph, is seen in the entire context to be integral to it — an explanation as to why Joseph had to go into Egypt to prepare the way for his family and give them opportunity to develop in isolation. It was becoming impossible for a single family group to dwell among the Canaanites and not be overwhelmed by their spreading moral rot. In Egypt, where they were segregated, they grew into a mighty nation. Even then, as later history proved, they could not withstand the Canaanite influence. Their incomplete obedience to God's command to exterminate the Canaanites became the seed of their own downfall.

That Israel was not completely obedient to God's command to destroy the Canaanites did not abrogate His judgment. It was only delayed a thousand years until the armies of Rome defeated Hannibal, the last great Canaanite leader. It was Canaanites who founded the important city of Carthage on the northern African coast. There they transported all their business acumen, seafaring skill, and moral depravity. They became the chief threat to the might of Rome. When Cato thundered in the Roman Senate, "Carthage must be destroyed!" he unknowingly echoed the decision of almighty God. The Punic Wars thus completed what the Conquest of Canaan in Joshua's time had begun.

The archaeological discoveries of recent years with the

interesting sidelights and parallels they throw on Old Testatment customs have led many scholars to the dangerous interpretation that the Hebrews borrowed their laws, their rituals, and even their festivals from the Canaanites. It is ridiculous to suggest, as has been done, that the Passover arose in Canaan as a somewhat disinfected version of the Canaanitish spring festival celebrating the release of man and beast from winter's bondage. Such an interpretation denies the fact that Passover began in Egypt, not Canaan, the night before the Israelites left the land of their bondage and it celebrates their deliverance. It ignores also God's concern that His people "shall not commit any of these abominations, neither any of your own nation, nor any stranger that sojourneth among you" (verse 26). The festivals which God ordered for His people were not outgrowths of corrupt Canaanite practice.[16]

In fact, though we have not discovered any Canaanite law codes, we have recovered many of their rituals. In character and intent, these are all vastly different from those of Israel. Canaanite rituals are performed, according to the Old Testament text, only when practiced by the apostate king and their followers. And it was against these that the prophets thundered.

Such Canaanite practices shed light on some of the strange customs of modern Jews. The thrice repeated command, "Thou shalt not seethe a kid in his mother's milk" (Exodus 23:19; 34:26; Deuteronomy 14:21) is the origin of the Jewish practice of keeping meat and milk so separate that they are cooked and eaten in separate sets of dishes — and even in separate kitchens in well-to-do-homes. Its meaning long defied interpreters who sometimes came up with such altruistic explanations as kindness to animals. Now we know that it was an important act in the Canaanite temple ritual and thus Israel was not to run the risk of practicing it.

THE RESPONSIBILITY OF THE CALLED

If anyone ever had reason to obey God implicitly, it was the Israelites. They knew they were no match for the Canaanites. God had made clear that it was inner corruption, not military weakness, that would be the cause of their downfall. He had given Israel detailed laws and commanded their complete separation from the heathen. They were to dwell apart in order to keep the pure knowledge of Jehovah alive on the earth and to become the channel of His redemption.

But Israel decided they were God's pet and that only the heathen need fear judgment. They accepted the privileges of being a chosen people and rejected the responsibilites. From the first they were a rebellious people — they began by sparing the Canaanites and continued by creating social ties with them, intermarrying with them, and joining them in worship. The first two chapters of Judges summarize the steps to their downfall. 1) Israel mixed socially and permitted intermarriage, thus backsliding toward the faith of the Canaanites; 2) the Lord's anger was kindled and He brought judgment or captivity upon them; 3) the people repented and called on the Lord again; 4) God heard and sent His deliverer. This dreary cycle is repeated generation after generation until even the deliverer Samson succumbed to the temptation of heathen women.

Later the kings, whom God intended to be shepherds and examples to the people, became the leaders who plunged them headlong to their destruction. Had God withheld judgment from them, no people would again have taken Him seriously. Again and again He warned them, but finally the Captivity came for the reasons detailed in II Kings 17.

God's honor was then at stake. He had sworn an oath to Abraham and to David concerning their seed, and so He could not utterly destroy Israel as He had the Canaanites, regardless of how deserving of it they might be. The Captivity was indeed a blessing — it purged Israel forever from the temptation to idolatry, and it made them zealous, once they were allowed to return, to keep heathen admixture from again diluting their distinctiveness.

God has not changed. No nation today, regardless of its wealth, or its influence, or its education, or its cultural resources, can afford to let moral decay sap its vitality. In fact, the greater a nation's blessings, privileges, or opportunity to know His word, the greater is that nation's responsibility to make godliness the core of its political and social philosophy. God still warns; He still gives many opportunities for repentance, but when He is persistently ignored or defied, the time eventually comes when He must say, "Thus far and no farther."

Nor is the church, as greatly as He loves her, immune from His judgment. She is destined to be His spotless bride. Thus, when she fails to uphold His standards or to witness to His holiness, whenever she degrades His Book to the level of man's wisdom and cheapens His love to the dotings of an elderly grandfather, then her Lord must act to uphold His integrity. Church history is the story of groups of Christians which were called into being and greatly blessed and used for a time; then, having become complacent and comfortable in their riches in this world, were set aside to watch another group rise up and carry on the testimony.

Good parents know that the truest love is not expressed by indulgence or permissiveness or by making excuses for bad behavior. The more loving the parent the more eager he is to instill habits of righteousness, to discipline, and to train, and the more careful he is to be sure his warnings against evil are taken seriously.

Yet the conscientious and loving parent does not enjoy punishing his child and always hopes to avoid it. So true is this that we often give far too many warnings before we carry one out. No less does our God hate judgment.

Sufficient evidence of this is seen in the great number of prophets He sent Israel and Judah during the three hundred years between Elijah and the Babylonian Captivity. How is it that thinking men can expect God to operate on a lower standard of justice than they demand of themselves, or can accuse Him of lacking love when He acts in a manner they themselves consider right?

The namby-pamby theology which teaches that a loving God could not possibly exercise discipline or punishment makes God less discerning than the most sensible parents. The God who loves defiant men so much that He was willing to enter the human race Himself and submit to the cruel abuse of their depravity did not let corruption run its full course. He has given us an example of the lengths to which evil can go in the days before the Flood when corruption spread so widely that only one man and his family were fit to be saved alive. Evil could have spread that widely again with the Canaanites dominating and influencing the world of that day. If God were to keep His chosen nation to transmit His message to the world and to produce His Messiah, He must protect it morally as well as physically from corrupting influences of surrounding heathen nations. The Canaanites were destroyed for the good of all mankind.

Those to whom God had given special privilege had special responsibility. Would He ever be taken seriously if Israel, of all people, had been allowed to reap the full results of disobedience? The Captivity came upon them in all its force because, as II Kings 17 reiterates in detail, they had disobeyed His commands and followed the ways of those they were supposed to destroy. Israel had ample warning of the danger of judgment for, as II Kings 17:13 reminded them, God had sent many prophets to call them to repentance. These prophets had been at best unheeded, at worst persecuted. The Captivity preserved Israel for God's purposes in history, and saved His plan of redemption for us all.

God does not delight in judgment. He calls it His "strange" work (Isaiah 28:21). It is not His will that any should perish, but He longs to bring all men to repentance (II Peter 3:9). But He will not allow any people, however great their material contributions to civilization and culture have been, to spread corruption unchecked. Neither will He allow His church, the carrier of His message today, to take on the ways of the world without facing chastisement (Hebrews 12:6). But He doesn't chastise with joy.

It is only in the Bible that we learn God is love; and it is only in the same Bible that we learn of what He decreed against the Canaanites. Perhaps we should ask, not "How could He destroy them?" but "How could He bear with them so long?" Rather than bemoan their fate, let us take heed to ourselves lest we fail to learn the lesson they provide.

FIG TREES AND IRON STONES
Evidence from Geography

Nelson Glueck had long been fascinated," says *Time's* cover story on him, "by a verse describing the Promised Land as a place 'whose stones are iron and out of whose hills thou mayest dig brass'" (Deuteronomy 8:9). Palestine was not noted for this metal but, continued *Time*, "Glueck trusted his Biblical Baedecker and kept looking for signs of ancient copper mining."[17]

Such trust in the geographical accuracy of the Bible has not always been characteristic of Bible scholars or critics. A popular high school text describes Palestine thus: "As a homeland, Canaan left much to be desired. It lacked fertile soil, natural resources and harbors . . . In spite of its drawbacks . . . they called it the 'land flowing with milk and honey'" because it was better than the desert in which they had been wandering.[18]

There are at least three things wrong with the above statement: 1) there is much evidence that the soil was more fertile and productive in ancient times than now; 2) we now know the land was rich in mineral resources; even in Solomon's day copper was smelted; and 3) in recent years we have excavated harbor towns used by the ancients. Perhaps we should say the statement has only one basic error — an easy one to make — namely, to argue that ancient conditions must have been like the modern: that because the land has been unproductive and underdeveloped in modern times (until 1948 and the emergence of the state of Israel), it was necessarily so in ancient times.

When the new state of Israel asked archaeologist Nelson Glueck to help them find water sources to support their fast increasing population, he crossed the country with Bible in hand. Wherever the Bible indicated that in ancient times a given spot had supplied a source of water, he ordered his workmen to dig. And where they dug, they struck water.

During the Arab-Israeli wars, the Israeli generals, Yigael Yadin and Moshe Dayan, used their knowledge of the land to achieve some notable exploits. Glueck attributes these achievements to their careful study of the military campaigns described in the Bible.[19] It is also said that General Allenby led the British forces to victory against the Turks at Megiddo in World War I by his Biblical knowledge of a trail that would permit him to attack their rear.

Two of these men — Yadin and Dayan are archaeologists as well as generals — have staked their archaeological careers on the accuracy of the Bible by using it for clues to indicate the spots where they should dig for lost knowledge of life in ancient times. Glueck calls the Bible his "divining rod."[20]

PHYSICAL GEOGRAPHY

When talking about the wanderings of the patriarchs, the wars of Israel, or the travels of Paul, the writers of Scripture must make many incidental references to such things as hills and valleys, streams and water holes, cities and deserts, foodstuffs and wildlife.

Taken together these provide us with a detailed picture of the natural and political features of ancient Palestine.

Its extensive ultimate boundaries were described by God to Moses on Mount Sinai (Exodus 23:31a). The reference here to the Mediterranean as the "Sea of the Philistines" is significant, suggesting as it does that the Philistines then dominated the sea rather than the seacoast of Philistia. The Egyptian records of the thirteenth and twelfth centuries B.C. refer to a number of "peoples of the sea," the most important of whom were the Philistines who came marauding the coast from the islands of the north. Thus the only reference the Bible makes to the Mediterranean by this name comes during the period when it is known (from other sources) that the Philistines were men of the sea harrying any poorly defended coast.

The desert mentioned in this verse is probably the wilderness to the south (today known by its Biblical name — the Negev), in which the Israelites wandered for forty years. In Scripture the River, or Great River, usually refers to the Euphrates. Except for a very brief period in the days of Solomon, Israel has never completely possessed these boundaries.

In Numbers 13:29, we have the report of the twelve spies Moses had sent to investigate the land promised to Israel. They came back with an accurate description of its topography in relation to peoples: "The Amalekites dwell in the land of the south [the Negev]: and the Hittites, and the Jebusites, and the Amorites, dwell in the mountain: and the Canaanites dwell by the sea, and by the coast of Jordan."

These twelve spies (Numbers 13:27) spoke of the Promised Land as flowing "with milk and honey" and brought back samples of its productivity. They also described high walled cities (verse 28). Archaeological excavation shows that the cities did stand high on tells (mounds built up by successive centuries of occupation and destruction) and were fenced by walls of gigantic construction.

Because Palestine has for the last few hundred years been arid and uninhabitable until the new state of Israel undertook its concentrated development, skeptics have laughed at a description of the area as a land "flowing with milk and honey," supporting a stable agriculture population, and abounding in plant and animal life.

Meanwhile, evidence has been collecting which suggests that a vast climatic change has come over the whole Near Eastern area in the past few thousand years. Drawings of hippopotami and giraffes on rocks in the Sahara indicate that water holes and trees must have once been characteristic of what is now earth's greatest desert. As recently as the first century A.D. the Negev — that vast southern portion of Palestine referred to in Scripture as "the south" or "the desert" — was heavily populated, as the New Testament suggests.

The prosperous first-century kingdom of the Nabateans stretched from the Sinai Peninsula and the Negev in the south up east of Jordan (east of Perea, Decapolis, and the Tetrarchy of Philip) as far as Damascus. It is the Arabia Paul referred to in Galatians 1:17. Its fabulous capital was the rose-colored city of Petra with its rock-hewn structures. Aretus IV (9 B.C. — A.D. 40), its king, sought Paul's life after his conversion and preaching stirred up the Jews in Damascus (Acts 9:22-25; II Corinthians 11:32). Although the rainfall even then must have been scanty (it now rarely exceeds six inches per year), it was carefully collected in numerous cisterns and reservoirs and used to irrigate lands that have since been reclaimed by the desert. Many of these have been found in recent times.[21]

The work of Nelson Glueck in particular is responsible for these finds and has shown us that the Negev has not experienced any major permanent climatic changes since the time of the Nabateans. It was wars and severe economic catastrophes rather than weather that explain the disappearance of the civilizations which once flourished there.

The land has been shown to be very fertile, lacking only water. We know now that the ancients knew how to make the most of the skimpy rainfall by not only catching it in the newly discovered cisterns but by making irrigation canals as well. As these cisterns and reservoirs are uncovered, they are being put back into use, for many are still watertight after all these centuries. Those ancient engineers might have something to teach our modern makers of swimming pools.

Evidence from archaeological sites substantiates the statement of Deuteronomy 8:7 that the land was better watered in ancient times than in recent. The Megiddo water system shows evidence of a lowering of the water table in that area. This would result from the cutting down of too many trees. By his discovery of the "upper and nether springs" (Judges 1:15) at Tell Beit Mirsim, M.G. Kyle identified the site with the ancient Debir given by Caleb to Othniel as his daughter's dowry.

Every city not only needed water to exist, but sought to deny any water outside its reach to potential besiegers. For this reason Hezekiah built the famous tunnel aqueduct of Siloam wich was found by a boy in 1880. The water would thus be brought into Jerusalem and denied to the Assyrian invaders (II Kings 20:20; II Chronicles 32:30).

Again in the matter of water, the "green and well-watered plain of Jordan," which tempted Lot to settle near Sodom, has come in for jeers in recent times. Evidence, however, shows that the land was once well-forested and that extensive over-cutting throughout the centuries of occupation had considerably lowered the water table. Tree-planting is one of the priority projects of the new Israel.

Not only were a large agricultural population and extensive herds possible in the land during Biblical times, but evidence both in and out of the Bible suggests that in ancient times wildlife was more numerous than now. The lists of clean and unclean animals in the Law (Leviticus 11) is suggestive. Lions and elephants are known to have at one time roamed there. In fact, the frequent mention of ivory (e.g. I Kings 22:39; Psalm 45:18) suggests that there was a good supply.

The spies whom Moses sent found pomegranates and figs and grapes so large that two men were needed to carry one bunch (Numbers 13:23). Wheat, barley, grapes and olives were staple crops. And what did Dr. Yadin find when he excavated Masada, the last stronghold of the Jews to fall to the Roman armies? The dehydrated remains of dates, walnuts, pomegranates, olive pits, and grain![22]

The story of the dramatic last stand of the Jewish revolt on Masada which rises mesa-like among the arid hills near the southwestern corner of the Dead Sea is told to us in vivid detail by Josephus in his *Antiquities of the Jews.* Yadin's discoveries have done much to vindicate Josephus' reputation as a careful historian.

That the land was both fertile and productive should not surprise us since the discovery has also been made that there actually were "stones of iron" and hills where they could "dig brass" (Deuteronomy 8:9). Palestine has not been considered a land of mineral wealth, but Professor Glueck could not get away from the verse in Deuteronomy 8:9 which describes it as "a land whose stones are iron, and out of whose hills thou mayest dig brass." Nelson Glueck made a list of ten Biblical reasons for his belief that copper might be found, probably in the south near the Gulf of Aqabah in the Wadi Arabah. In what many regard as those dull genealogies of First Chronicles, he was puzzled by I Chronicles 4:14 that names a "valley of Charashim [smiths]" and I Chronicles 4:12 that refers to "Irnahash [a city of copper]."[23] Then, Moses had raised the brazen serpent (Numbers 21:4-11) somewhere near the northern end of the Gulf of

Aqabah, probably in the Arabah rift valley.[24] Drawing these brief references together, Glueck decided to explore the Arabah Valley for signs of ancient copper smelting.[25]

While searching, he was told by some Arabs of a place called Khirbet Nahas (ruin of copper). As his expedition approached it, they immediately recognized copper slag heaps and discovered small stone ovens for smelting the ore. From pottery fragments lying about, it was immediately possible to date the site in the time of King Solomon. And, Glueck adds: "The mineral deposits of the Wadi Arabah are far from exhausted. On the contrary, it seems that they have hardly been scratched despite intensive mining of the ores carried on there" [26] in Old Testament times.

POLITICAL GEOGRAPHY

Not only were the Biblical descriptions of the natural geography of Bible lands — that is, land contours, natural resources, flora and fauna — completely accurate as to its condition in ancient times, but the political features of the ancient Near East have readily revealed themselves to those who sought them out by using the Bible as their guidebook. Whenever the Scripture refers to cities or empires or other man-made boundaries, or to people and government, the historians, archaeologists and anthropologists, picking up their trails, find them to be just as described. From the air the tracks of the ancient caravan routes can still be traced in the land. The trails of Abraham can be followed. Naturally many peoples traversed the land and a number of them settled there.

We have already discussed the ancient Hurrian (Biblical Horite) kingdom which flourished in Northern Mesopotamia and opened its secrets to us with the discovery of the Mari tablets. This kingdom fell under the domain of the Hittites who had one of the great empires of ancient times, but who so completely disappeared from history that Bible references to them were laughed off because the Bible made them sound like a mighty people, whereas if they existed at all they "obviously" must have been quite insignificant. Since the exciting discovery of the ancient Hittite capital of Boghazkoy, the Hittite Empire is now given its rightful place in the history textbooks.

It is not surprising that Numbers 13:28-29 names so many different peoples as living in Palestine. We have seen already how the situation of the land made it the crossroads of the ancient world.

The Philistines, already mentioned in connection with their crossing the sea from Greece, belonged to it, not as natives but as near conquerors. During the days of the Judges they established themselves in five strong cities — Ashdod, Ashkelon, Ekron, Gath and Gaza. From time to time they asserted their authority over Israel, humbling such leaders as Samson, Eli and Saul. It was not until David was king that Israel was finally and permanently victorious over the Philistines. However, it was the Philistines who gave their name — Palestine — to the territory.

This accurate reflection of a knowledge of ancient peoples extends even as far back as the fascinating Table of Nations in Genesis 10. Says Dr. William Albright of this list: "Scholars never fail to be impressed with the author's knowledge of the subject."[27]

It was the great fortified, walled cities of the Canaanites which most impressed ten of the spies whom Moses had sent into the land. We know it was customary for settled peoples of that day to build their cities on high places commanding a view and fortress advantage of the countryside in order to repel invaders. The high stone walls around the cities made them appear even more formidable to all but the eye of faith.

Even so, they were from time to time invaded, burned, or in other ways fell into disuse. Later settlers would level off the rubble of the past and build on it. Over the centuries the effect was to build the "tells," as these mounds were called, higher and higher. The sites of these ancient cities are reflected in the names of many modern communities throughout the Near East: Tell Beit Mirsim, Tell en Nasbeh, Tell el Husn, and a large number of others. Archaeologists find the history of a given site by digging down into these tells to uncover the various layers of occupation — the lowest level being the most ancient.

The archaeologists have found that wherever the Book of Joshua claims that a city was conquered, they find a city in a level dating to Joshua's time that shows evidence of having undergone violent destruction. Wherever Joshua mentions a city that he did not conquer, the proper level of occupation of that city also agrees with his statement. These latter are the cities mentioned in Joshua 11:13 as "standing in their strength." The King James Bible translators did not have the advantage of archaeological findings to understand the meaning of the Hebrew word *tell*, which is used only in Joshua 11:13. A literal rendering of the passage would be "stood on their tells."

There was also the mention of a port on the Red Sea in Solomonic times. This, too, roused Glueck's curiosity. It is first mentioned as a stop on the route of the wilderness wanderings (Numbers 33:35-36; Deuteronomy 2:8). Its importance as a city, however, first appears in Solomon's time (I Kings 9:26) and it is also the seaport near which the fleet of Jehoshaphat foundered on rocks, before it could set sail to Ophir (I Kings 22:48). Believing a local legend, explorers had sought it some twenty-five to thirty-five kilometers from the sea, but Glueck's excavation in Tell Khaleifeh confirmed this small site close to the gulf as the lost ancient port of Solomon and, as he called it, the "Pittsburgh of Palestine."

Although at first the site seemed most undesirable because it lay in the direct path of winds that come constantly down the Arabah rift, excavation revealed that it was built to take best advantage of these winds, making its ovens blast furnaces to complete the smelting of copper begun up in the valley. The town was built completely new on virgin soil and according to a preconceived plan.

For Solomon to have built it must have required much careful planning and supplying. Many caravans must have carried the multitude of craftsmen, shipbuilders and slaves needed for the enterprise. The result was the seaport of Ezion-Geber from which he shipped out his copper in return for the exotic goods of faraway ports, including those of the land of the Queen of Sheba.[28] "There was," Glueck says, "only one man who possessed the strength, wealth and wisdom capable of initiating and carrying out such a highly complex and specialized undertaking. He was King Solomon."[29] It is a unique confirmatory evidence of the wisdom of Solomon and his marvels (I Kings 10).

Ophir has also been the subject of speculation. Not only did Solomon obtain gold, silver, and precious stones there in exchange for his copper, but we are told he received monkeys, peacocks, sandalwood (almug trees) and ivory (I Kings 10:11,22). It now appears that the Hebrew words used in these verses for these items are all derived from Indian roots, which has brought Richard D. Barnett of the British Museum to conclude: "Was Ophir perhaps not imaginary — a fanciful legend of the narrator? At Qusile, near Jaffa in Israel, a sherd of the eighth century B.C. inscribed 'gold of Ophir for Beth-horon: 30 shekels' was recently discovered . . . . This shows Ophir was not just a fairyland — a myth invented by the Biblical narrator. Ophir was probably the ancient city of Suppara near Bombay."[30]

Cities mentioned in the days of the kings and of the Captivity (particularly Babylon and Shushan), the Galilean towns where Jesus visited, and the cities where Paul journeyed have all been subjected to similar investigation. In no instance has anything contrary to Scripture been uncovered, and sometimes there are thrilling confirmations.

In recent years skin divers and underwater archaeologists have been making remarkable discoveries in the port of Caesarea built by Herod. Although in ancient times ships were small enough to be hauled up on almost any beach, ports provided protection in times of storm were much preferred. Herod improved Caesarea by the construction of a great circular mole (a breakwater), the remains of which can still be seen from the air under the blue waters of the Mediterranean. Herod commemorated his work by striking coins that pictured the entrance to his sheltered harbor. [31] That the ancients had no use for harbors of the magnitude of those needed for modern great ocean-going transports was completely overlooked by the textbook writers mentioned earlier who described the Promised Land as lacking harbors.

The primary purpose of the Bible is not, of course, to teach the geography of Palestine, yet no more reliable textbook of geography could be written. Says Nelson Glueck: "The boundaries of entire lands and the nature of their ancient civilizations can be made clear by following clues in the Bible. It is almost as if one waves a magic wand over a blank area of the earth, and it becomes filled with roads, cities, people, and all the paraphernalia of throbbing life."[32]

WHO HAS THE ANSWERS . . .
Naturalistic Scientists or Bible Writers?

I can't believe the Bible; it's full of scientific errors."
How often this kind of remark issues from those who
don't want to believe! The challenge to the scientific
accuracy of Scripture has been so frequent in our time
that many believers have retreated from the fray and
fallen back to this position: "The Bible is, after all, not a
textbook of science, but rather of religion." They
emphasize that its purpose is to acquaint us with the
Creator and that references to His creation are incidental.

But does this dodge really settle matters so easily? Are
we not instead faced with the problem which F. Alton
Everest raised in his Preface to *Modern Science and the
Christian Faith:* "Surely if the Book is found
untrustworthy in these incidental contacts, the spiritual
message might be viewed with suspicion."[33]

Undoubtedly the Zeus[34] of the twentieth-century
world is science, and the scientist is his high priest. The
scientist by mere virtue of his calling is listened to with
respect on any subject on which he chooses to
pronounce, be it human relations, politics, or religion.
Modern critics of the Bible, therefore, demand that the
Bible line up with the latest scientific thinking.

However, the "latest scientific thinking" changes so fast that ten-year-old textbooks are obsolete, whereas the Bible presents truth that has stood the test of the centuries. Critics seem to make an unreasonable demand on Scripture. Nevertheless, for those who have been taught that the Bible is unscientific, it is possible to demonstate that it has never been shown contrary to any provable *fact* of science.

MAN'S STATUS BEFORE GOD

Dr. Henry Morris, who is doing as much to uphold the scientific accuracy of the Bible for this generation as Harry Rimmer did for students of the thirties, has written an article whose title flatly proclaims: "The Bible is A Textbook of Science."[35] By this he does not mean that it is organized in the manner of a modern scientific textbook or that it gives detailed technical descriptions or mathematical formulae, for it does not. He means that wherever it touches on a subject capable of experimental verification it has not been proven false. Its remarks concerning natural phenomena and historic events must be included in the total body of objective data. After all, as Job discovered, it is not God or His Word that is on trial, but man as he stands before God.

God answered Job's spiritual problems by showing him how little he knew of natural things. Job accepted God's omniscience and trusted Him for the spiritual answers. Today we try to bring God's Word down to the level of our knowledge.

When the "conflict between science and Scripture" is referred to, most people think of the conflict between the theory of evolution and the Genesis account of creation. For a century after the publication of Darwin's *"Origin of Species"* in 1859, the quarrel between scientists and theologians was bitter. Today, however, it is popular to pretend no conflict exists. The highly acclaimed little book, *Seven Reasons Why A Scientist*

Believes in God,[36] is an evidence of this trend. The title sounds very nice, but the work is a lengthy statement that purports to show how the processes of evolution strengthen belief in a Designer. That the concept of evolution contradicts the Word of the Designer concerning His creation appears not to matter to the author.

Christians have also been too eager to reconcile the contradictions — usually by taking scientific conclusions at face value and explaining away the plain meaning of the words of Scripture only to have the scientific position shift and be compelled to start a new reconciliation.

It is impossible in a limited space to demonstrate either the fallacies of the evolutionary theory or the difficulty of harmonizing it with Biblical creation. Henry Morris has convincingly summarized the Biblical position in *The Twilight of Evolution.*[37] It warrants careful study by everyone interested in pursuing the subject.

Evolution, however, is not the only area of interaction between Scripture and science. One noteworthy aspect is the fact that, unlike other ancient literature, the Bible never makes the mistake of endorsing the scientific errors common to its time of writing. It has shown itself to be well in advance of mere human knowledge. For example, when men believed the earth was flat, they could have read Isaiah 40:22 and learned it was round.

But men have always sought to make the Bible fit their preconceptions. Probably the most famous example of this was the trial of Galileo, the early seventeenth-century Italian astronomer and physicist who has been called the founder of modern experimental science. In an age that believed the earth was the center of the universe (the geocentric theory), Galileo had not only accepted the Copernican heliocentric theory (that the sun is the center of the solar system), but ably demonstrated it with his telescope and pen. For this he was, in 1633, hauled before the courts of the Inquisition. The attack on

Galileo began with a sermon on the text, "Why stand ye gazing up into heaven?" (Acts1:11), which in itself shows how texts can be rent out of context to prove anything.

Galileo attempted to show that the Scriptures often use figurative language when speaking of natural phenomena, as indeed we all do. However, convinced of the traditional theory, the Inquisitors condemned his writing as heresy, claiming that Scriptures like Joshua 10:12 and Ecclesiastes 1:5 taught that the sun, not the earth, moved. Today we recognize the Ecclesiastes passage as an instance of figurative language still common among us, and the Joshua passage has a variety of alternatives.[38]

Ignorance is the basis of most scientific attacks on the Bible. For instance, late in the last century the notorious infidel, Robert Ingersoll, gave a popular lecture entitled "Some Mistakes of Moses" in which he claimed to find more than fifty scientific fallacies in the Pentateuch. Since they were based on superficial knowledge of the text, they were easily refuted even then by scholars. But they still appeal to the shallow mind that wants to defy God's Word, and so they are from time to time resurrected. Typical examples are the *arabeth* and *shaphan* said to chew the cud in Leviticus 11. Though translated respectively "hare" and "coney" by the King James Version, Hebrew scholars do not know what the words mean. Nobody knows what the *arabeth* was since the word is not used in any other known writing. It is certainly not to be equated with the English "hare" which admittedly does not chew its cud. Moses said the *arabeth*, whatever it was, did chew the cud and we have no reason to doubt his word. The *shaphan* is probably a member of the pig family abundant in the Near East four thousand years ago but now extinct. Fossil teeth suggest it may very well have chewed its cud.

It is hard to imagine a better way of deflating scientific ego than by giving a few scientists the test God gave Job.

Job, in his suffering and confusion, had sought to confront God and receive vindication from Him. In chapter 38, we read how God granted this request and in so doing, demonstrated the truth of Job's earlier statement: "Behold, the fear of the Lord, that is wisdom; and to depart from evil is understanding" (Job 28:28). Job had been asking some hard questions — questions on the meaning of human suffering that men still ask. Then it was God's turn. His questions were whoppers!

Job had dared to question God's treatment of him and God answers in effect: "I'm the One to do the asking. How little you really know! Could you create this world? Were you around to see how I did it?" (Job 38:3,4). It is a good question to ask the evolutionist who dares to proclaim the Genesis account inaccurate. Evolution has no answers concerning creation. No matter how far back the theory is carried, eventually there comes a point when the scientist must say to the first molecule, "Where did you come from?"

Most all peoples have some form of creation story. W.F. Albright, however, calls the Genesis account "unique in ancient literature. It undoubtedly reflects an advanced monotheistic point of view, with a sequence of creative phrases which is so rational that modern science cannot improve on it, given the same language and the same range of ideas in which to state its conclusions. In fact, modern scientific cosmogonies show such a disconcerting tendency to be short-lived that it may be seriously doubted whether science has yet caught up with the Biblical story."[39]

Of course the Holy Spirit used non-technical language. He did not write the Bible for twentieth-century scientists alone but for all men of all ages. He is simple enough for the most unlearned, profound enough that the deepest student never exhausts His meaning, and accurate enough that the most learned cannot catch Him in error.

God next queried Job concerning the natural phenomena of the world around him (Job 38:16-30). Turning Job's eyes to the heavens, He continued with even more searching questions (verses 31-38). It is interesting to realize that many of God's questions would still be unanswered even by specialists. Notice that Job did not even attempt to answer. While he was still pondering these questions, the Lord threw out another barrage, this time concerning the habits and traits of a number of animals (Job 38:39—39:30).

When Job remained silent, God tried another subject: "How about the relationships between the earth, atmosphere, and heavens? Can you explain that?" We have made a little advance in this area since Job's day, but those who know most about it are the quickest to admit that vast areas still await our understanding.

As chapter 40 opens, God paused to demand an answer of Job: "Shall he that contendeth with the Almighty instruct Him? He that reproveth God, let him answer it" (verse 2). How applicable to modern faultfinders! And how easy to be a faultfinder — to become puffed up in our own pretentious ignorance. Today's critics base their charges on unproven theories and construed conclusions that may overstate the facts.

Job knew when he was beaten, and being a very wise and God-fearing man, replied, "I will lay my hand upon my mouth" (verse 4). Job was not wise in his own conceits. He knew that nobody could bluff God.

When Job began to listen instead of talk, the Lord took His opportunity to drive home the lesson. His earlier sets of questions had demonstrated to Job's satisfaction the limits of human knowledge and the vastness of the divine. The Lord then showed him that, despite the fact that man was commanded to rule the earth, he had shown himself incapable of doing so. Man, who was intended to subdue the earth (Genesis 1:28), had fallen far short of succeeding. Two of the animals, the hippopotamus (behemoth, Job 40:15-24) and the crocodile (leviathan, Job 41:1), which He singled out for special comment, remain to this day untamed for any purpose of man.

Job made no attempt to reply. He admitted he did not know the answers and rested content with the superior knowledge of his God. It is not necessary that we have a complete explanation of everything God has said and done before we accept His Word. It is sufficient to know that in the explosion of scientific learning nothing has shown any Biblical statement contrary to fact. With our present knowledge we may not be able to prove every scientific statement in the Bible true, but we cannot prove any untrue.

In the early forties Harry Rimmer was sued for a thousand dollars. The one bringing suit claimed to have fulfilled an offer Rimmer made to pay that sum for proof of a scientific error in the Bible. After a day and a half the case was thrown out of court for lack of evidence. The plaintiff's charges amounted to a revival of Ingersoll's "Mistakes of Moses," which have been frequently answered. Furthermore, in New York City with all its institutions of learning and research the plaintiff had not found a single scientist to appear in court in his favor.[40]

To try to harmonize every scientific theory with Scripture is a waste of time, effort and paper. What reams of paper were used to show that Genesis could be made to agree with the now discredited nebular hypothesis![41]

Man's position before God is that of a suppliant, a learner, a listener. God has the answers, and in His Word and through His works He deigns to reveal some of them.

MAN'S RESPONSE TO GOD

Man's response to God depends not so much on his learning as on his basic attitude. In recent years this has been clearly demonstrated in the similar experiences of the Russian cosmonauts and American astronauts. All are capable men, trained to the highest possible degree. Yet the Russians who returned from their first venture into outer space boasted gleefully of the fact that they did not see God up there. On the other hand, a number of the Americans have spoken with utmost reverence of renewed appreciation for the greatness of the Creator. No one who heard it will forget how Frank Borman read the first chapter of Genesis to the millions listening on earth.

Like Job faced with the omniscience of God, every man must make some response. It has ever been Satan's desire to lead him into the wrong one. To Adam and Eve he said in effect: "You don't need God; you only need more knowledge. Get it and you can get along without Him" (Genesis 3:5).

Likewise, the "God is dead" theologians bolster their positions by alluding to "modern scientific thinking" and say that the idea of a personal God who involves Himself in the affairs of earth is an "archaic anthropomorphism[42] of a pre-scientific age."

Twentieth-century man lets scientific knowledge keep him from God, because he wants to be independent of God. A physiologist, questioned by reporters who were surprised because he had defended miracles at a medical convention, had this to say: "Most scientists are not Christians, but not because they're scientists. Most businessmen or most reporters are not Christians either; in fact, most people are not Christians."[43] He then gave a ringing testimony to the miracle of the new birth in his life. Here was a man scientifically educated but humble in his knowledge and grateful for the privilege of thinking God's thoughts after Him.

The fact is that man in his arrogance insists on finding God with the use of his five physical senses — all he has by which to obtain knowledge. (Microscopes and similar tools are, after all, only methods of extending and refining the senses.) But God may be apprehended only by the spiritual sense which the unsaved man does not possess. Knowledge of God beyond what His creation reveals of Him can come to man only by revelation. The wisest man on earth cannot "by searching find out God" (Job 11:7).

Job's response to God's revelation was one of utter humility. This is the very opposite of those of whom the Scripture says, "knowledge puffeth up" (I Corinthians 8:1), and who demonstrate the fact by daring to question the Almighty.

But Job's humility was not the obnoxious Uriah Heep variety which takes pride in its humbleness. It was the humility of a truly great man who comes face to face with ultimate greatness. It was a humility based on gratitude; this is the only true humility.

It is man's pride which says, "I will believe only what I can demonstrate. I demand that God reveal Himself only on my terms," The one who approaches the study of natural phenomena in gratitude to God for a curious mind capable of learning and for health and energy to pursue knowledge is the one truly humble and truly able to absorb and use knowledge.

Job's response to God was also a response of faith. Though the troubles that generated his questions were still with him, he was now content to leave them in God's hands. Since human knowledge cannot encompass God, He must simply be trusted. Apart from faith, our greatest reach of knowledge can never comprehend God. Our Lord pointed this out to the Pharisees who had proved so blind to His claims (Matthew 16:1-4). "You think you are pretty knowledgeable," He told them, "because you are good weather prophets. You can read the physical omens in the sky. But when it comes to the signs of the times, you are utterly blind."

Science by itself is neither the friend nor the foe of faith. A few years ago two hundred leading scientists were asked whether they considered modern developments in science were favorable or unfavorable to religious faith. The replies were noncommital responses, probably not much different from what might have been found in a more typical general population sampling. For the one who has found God through His written revelation, whether he be scientist or apprentice, chemist or cook, will see Him in all that he touches, whereas the one who keeps his spiritual eyes fast shut will not see Him anywhere.

No scientific error has ever been proved against Scripture. What the Bible does not say as well as what it does say are in accord with fact. But as long as men prefer to ignore God's message, they will excuse themselves by claiming to see errors in the revelation. Christians will never be able to answer all the charges of unbelievers. Even scientists cannot do this, for the field of knowledge is so vast that each man would have to become a specialist in only one small area. There is a difference between not having information to prove a thing true, and having information to prove it false. No one has the latter information against the Bible. If there *appears* to be a discrepancy between the Book and the facts, the Christian will believe the Book because God has said it and because he knows that when all the evidence is in, the Scriptures cannot be broken.

It does not honor one's faith to have a cowardly fear of scientific facts. In the final analysis truth is the friend, not the foe, of Christianity (John 8:32). It was such fear of science that motivated the persecutors of Galileo. We are told of two leading churchmen who were invited to look into his telescope and see for themselves what Galileo was talking about. One refused for fear of seeing something upsetting to his belief; the other looked and then wrote to Rome asking whether he should call what he saw reality or only an illusion.

It was not primarily for asking for a sign that Jesus condemned the Pharisees (Matthew 16:1-3; Luke 12:54-56), but for refusing to accept His mighty works as signs. When John the Baptist sent his disciples to ask if He was really the promised One, Christ's only reply was that they go and show John His works (Matthew 11:2-6; Luke 7:19-23).

When Nicodemus — admittedly a learned man — complained because he could not understand what Jesus was talking about, he was rebuked (John 3:12): "If I tell you earthly things and ye believe not, how shall ye believe if I tell you heavenly things?"

A wise man once said, "It isn't the things in the Bible I can't understand that bother me. It's the things I can understand." God has told us in His Word all we need to know about our hopelessness and our lostness and our helplessness. He has told us about His love and His provision to make of us His sons and daughters. Shall we throw all this away because someone puffed up with a little learning tells us he has caught Almighty God in error? Or shall we believe that the truth which has withstood all previous attacks will prevail.

Like Job, our last word to God should be one of repentance for our doubts and questions.

7

MYTH, MAGIC OR MIRACLE ?
Some Supernatural Evidence

A group of men were out rowing on the Sea of Galilee when suddenly one rose excitedly, almost upsetting the boat. "Now I see it!" he exclaimed. "Now I know how Jesus walked on the water. See how it ripples lightly over the shallows there? Jesus could have walked almost out to our boat here and yet appeared to have been walking on the surface of the water." This is the attitude toward miracles we encounter today. The trend is to find a natural explanation for each one, then claim to "accept" it.

Such thinking is as shallow as the water this man saw. He did not reflect that the disciples could also have seen if the water was shallow. Neither did he recall that the occasion in question was a stormy night with high waves (Matthew 14:22-33; John 6:18-20).

In his well-known novel, *The Robe*, Lloyd C. Douglas gives us another example of this sort of anti-supernatural bias. He has the miracles of the five loaves and two fishes described by one of the five thousand present for the occasion. This "eyewitness" tells how the sight of a boy giving his meager lunch to the Lord so shamed him for his selfishness, that he brought his own hidden lunch out and shared it with others. Then he noticed that many people were doing the same thing to the extent that there was sufficient for the entire company. Such an explanation is a travesty on the power of the Creator who made the grain and the fish in the first place!

THE GOD OF NATURE

It used to be that these supernatural manifestations were considered among the most important evidences of the truth of the Christian faith, proving that it bore the stamp of authenticity from God Himself. As Nicodemus, a learned scholar, said to Jesus, "No man can do these miracles that thou doest except God be with him" (John 3:2).

A.H. Strong defines a miracle as "An event in nature, so extraordinary in itself and so coinciding with the prophecy or command of a religious teacher or leader, as fully to warrant the conviction, on the part of those who witness it, that God has wrought it with the design of certifying that this teacher or leader has been commissioned by him."[44]

Today the presence of the supernatural is embarrassing to those theologians who insist that faith must be in accord with man's reason and scientific advancement. They consider anything supernatural a major drawback to acceptance of the Christian faith. By seeking natural explanations for every supernatural occurrence, they rob Scripture of its character as the revelation of an omniscient and omnipotent God.

Of course, a natural explanation for a miracle is essential to anyone whose starting premise excludes the supernatural. Such an explanation is nothing but an effort to justify a rejection of the intervention of God into the affairs of men. As a professor of Old Testament Hebrew once scribbled on the margin of a student's paper, "It is not a question of whether God could do it, but whether He did do it." So far as that professor was concerned, God didn't.

Elijah certainly had no doubt but that his God was a God of miracles — one who had control of the elements of nature. So far as Elijah was concerned, God not only could but did.

The struggle between Jehovah and Baal did not begin when Elijah called the priests of Baal to Mount Carmel, but rather three and a half years earlier, on that bright day when a then unknown prophet dressed in skins suddenly appeared before Ahab, king of Israel, to announce: "As the Lord God of Israel liveth, before whom I stand, there shall not be dew nor rain these years, but according to my word" (I Kings 17:1).

This dramatic announcement is our first introduction to Elijah. Probably Ahab, too, had not heard of him before. This unknown had the audacity to stand before a king whose might was known throughout the world of his day. Shalmaneser III, king of Assyria, on his famous Black Obelisk describing his battle with the kings of the west (Syria and Palestine), lists Ahab third in power out of a dozen. And, according to Shalmaneser's figures, Ahab contributed more chariots — 2,000 — to the battle than did the first two kings put together. But Elijah did not fear Ahab nor his wife's prophets. He knew that Jehovah was God.

Baal was recognized by the Canaanites as the storm god whose resuscitation ushered in each rainy season. Ahab had married Jezebel, daughter of Ethbaal, king of Sidon, a Canaanite (Phoenician) city. Following his marriage he "went and served Baal, and worshiped him" (I Kings 16:31). More than that, because of Jezebel's influence Israel was in danger of having Baal worship become her state religion.

No more fitting challenge could have been hurled at the imposter Baal and his priests than that of withholding rain. Palestine is a land of two seasons — a wet and a dry one. The God who had the power to change that cycle would be the one who had instituted it. The three and one half years of closed heavens take on an added significance when we understand the normal alternating seasons (James 5:17).

It is possible that Elijah presented his challenge at the very season when the followers of Baal expected their god in the normal course of events to bring in the annual rains. It is interesting to calculate that three and one half years later when the rains did come, they came at the normal beginning of the *dry* season. Thus Jehovah demonstrated that He is the God who controls nature.

Both the spectacular manifestations of the prophets and the miracles of Jesus have been explained away as mythological additions to the basic historical facts. Now, myths are generally understood as stories whose origin is forgotten and whose purpose is to explain some natural phenomenon or belief or practice. To materialistic critics all evidences of supernatural power are to be taken as mythological, and they seek to demythologize (that is, remove these mythical elements) the Scriptures in order to get back to what residue of fact is buried under it. They may say that while Elijah was preaching against Jezebel's religion, there was a dry spell which he said they deserved. When it was prolonged, his followers built up the story that Elijah was responsible for it.

This method has been applied to the Gospels by critics until there seems to be nothing of real fact left. One historian, accepting such thinking, flatly says, "Just what Jesus did preach . . . historians cannot determine fully."[45]

Yet a broadminded Jewish scholar of Jerusalem says, "If skeptical and hairsplitting criticism like this were applied to the historical sources for the life and views of Charlemagne or Mohammed, we should not have left of them anything of even relative historical validity except their mere existence."[46]

The miracles of the Old Testament are discredited

even more blatantly on the assumption that previous to the great preaching prophets (who are supposed to be the first to have given a monotheistic and lofty ethical concept of religion) the human race was in a childhood of intelligence which made it gullible to fancy stories and clever tricksters.

But the liberal theologian turns the Biblical miracles into a form of magic; that is, the control of the supernatural by humans who know the right words or ceremonies to compel the spirits to obey. The lamp is rubbed just so and the genie must appear. On this assumption Elijah would have controlled the rainfall by combining as astute knowledge of weather forecasting with an incantation or ceremony which the supernatural spirit of the rain could not ignore.

It was such a concept which caused the ancient Jewish commentators to explain the miracles of Jesus (a good indication, by the way, that they could not deny they happened) by saying He stole from the high priest the pronunciation of the secret name of Jehovah and used this name to work His wonders.

Biblical miracles, however, are never an attempt of man to compel God to do his bidding. In every instance they are initiated by God Himself with the intent of compelling man to pay attention to Him. They are an essential element in the progressive development of God's revelation and the credentials that identify His messengers.

Just as no foreign ruler is expected to accept anyone as official spokesman for the government of a given country until that spokesman has first presented flawless credentials showing he was appointed in that capacity, so our Lord did not expect man to heed everyone who claimed to speak in His name but only those who could validate their claim by proper credentials. Thus, when Moses objected that the Israelites would "not believe me, nor hearken unto my voice; for they will say the

Lord hath not appeared unto thee" (Exodus 4:1), God resorted to the miraculous — the rod that became a serpent and the hand that became leprous. These signs, He said, would convince the people.

"But," the rationalist objects, "God who created the laws of nature would have more respect for His own law than to break it lightly and easily. In a less scientific age it was easier to believe in irrational forces in nature, but we know better now." Actually, man was no more gullible then, no less aware of the essential orderliness of nature than he is now. If the world had seemed disorganized and without rhyme or reason instead of a place governed by predictable orderliness, no miracles would have been recognized; anything would have gone.

It is like saying that God is always limited to operating the mechanics of the universe in the same way. Must the designer of an automobile always drive it forward because that is how it is normally expected to travel? The designer knew circumstances would arise to make it desirable to drive in reverse and so he engineered into it the ability to go in reverse if necessary without throwing the whole machinery into chaos. It is nice to know when you turn on a piece of machinery that it can be depended upon to operate in an expected way. It is also nice to know that when circumstances make it desirable, you can bring reverse gears into operation and make it do something different without harming the machine. This shows only that the machine is under the control of a superior intelligence whose needs it serves.

If the God of this creation has some seldom used power by which He can alter the usual pattern of nature's working, why should we assume that its use would reduce the orderly operation of the universe to chaos? Why assume that Almighty God would be less meticulous in His plans than a man? As a driver may slow down or honk to attract the attention of a pedestrian, so when God wants to attract attention, He may intervene in a *way that shows He is there. To get Israel's attention, He altered the weather cycle so that the rain did not fall at its expected season. Miracles consisted of something sufficiently unusual to attract man's attention and reveal something of God to him.*

We recognize that the Lord often does use natural forces in the performance of His miracles. The miracle, as often as not, consists in the timing and in the purpose. The waters of the Jordan have been known to cease flowing when an earthquake or some other natural phenomenon causes a bank to collapse and dam the flow temporarily. The miracle consisted of their ceasing when the feet of the priests bearing the Ark of the Covenant stepped into the water (Joshua 3) or when Elijah struck the water with his mantle (II Kings 2:8,14).

When the Red Sea parted as Moses raised his rod in obedience to God's command the waters separated — not too soon, not too late. The plagues of Egypt occurred at the moment Moses called for them. If, as it is popular to suggest, an earthquake toppled the walls of Jericho, it too was a miracle of timing, occurring as it did immediately after the seventh march around the city on the seventh day of the siege (Joshua 6).

The Lord Jesus demonstrated the control of God the Son over the elements of nature by walking on the water in which Peter, attempting to imitate Him sank and was in danger of drowning. (So much for the water being shallow that night!) Again, concerning Christ we read that the wind and the waves abated at His command (Mark 4:37-41). The disciples who witnessed His power recognized with great awe the miraculous.

Our God is in control, not only of the inanimate forces of nature, but of all living things as well. There have been efforts to explain the ravens which fed Elijah as being a tribe of bedouins known by that name. But this is not the only instance where God used animals to do His bidding. Job was reminded by God that man had not yet subdued all animals, but they are not beyond God's control! We have it on record that God stopped the mouths of lions, taught a jackass to talk back to its master, and safely rode an unbroken colt into Jerusalem. Without human guidance, some oxen bore the Ark of the Covenant back to Israel after it had been stolen. One creature of the sea swallowed and regurgitated a prophet on command, another produced tax money on schedule, and a whole school of them swam into a net when they were so ordered.

The God of the Bible has revealed Himself so completely as the God of all living matter that His control is shown to extend even to the causes of illness and death, as witnessed by the miracles of healing and raising of the dead. It would seem, in fact, that everything in creation obeys the will of the Creator except those whom He has chosen to subdue it and exercise dominion over it.

THE GOD OF HISTORY

The God of the Bible is the God of history, the Guide of the course of human events. God is interested in man. He has a plan for man that He is working out in spite of rebellion and opposition. He sought first and worked through a nation that would preserve His message and bring forth His Redeemer. Then He worked through a church that would spread His truth and be the fulfillment of His plans. At every crisis in the destiny of these two institutions — the nation and the church — miracles clustered to attest His power and His interest.

It is a mistake to picture life in the ancient world as being dotted with vagrant miracles that threw the inhabitants into confusion and left them wondering whether there was any order or predictability in the world. Such is far from the case, for God, as we have seen, is no celestial magician seeking to amuse or bewilder an appreciative audience. To quote B.B. Warfield:

"Miracles do not appear on the page of Scripture vagrantly, here, there, and elsewhere indifferently, without assignable reason. They belong to revelation periods, and appear only when God is speaking to His people through accredited messengers, declaring His gracious purposes."[47]

Because miracles appear only when God is speaking to His people through accredited messengers to declare His purposes, the only soberly attested miracles in history are associated with the Jews, with Christ, and with the founding of the church. God chose the Jews as His messengers to all men, and He had to so accredit them that those who refused to listen would be without excuse. Even among them the miracles were not lavish but assigned to critical periods. They cluster around Abraham who was to found the nation, around Moses who was to deliver and organize it, around Elijah who was to stem the inroads of heathenism and inaugurate the company of prophets who would reveal God's blueprint for history.

If history and human existence have meaning, they must be going somewhere. Without purpose and direction all life is meaningless. Man is utterly lost and without direction unless God reveals His purposes to us. And if He does have a goal for human history, our own individual existence can have meaning only if we are in line with it. Thus, when men have spoken to reveal God's plans, they have demonstrated that they possessed God's power.

So it is only to be expected that at the great focal point of history — that time described by the prophets for which all previous history had been preparing and from which all subsequent history flows — the greatest miracles should cluster.

Elijah and Elisha, whose utterances were miraculously attested, lived in a period of grave crisis for the chosen nation. The Northern Kingdom had gone far into apostasy which started when its first king, Jeroboam, set up a separate center of worship in defiance of God's revealed will (compare Deuteronomy 12 with I Kings 12:25-33). Under Ahab's strong-willed wife, a heathen religion was becoming predominant and enforced by state sanction. The worship of Jehovah was pushed so far underground that at one point Elijah thought he alone was faithful (I Kings 19:4-18). Apostasy's evil tentacles were reaching at Judah.

Although the Southern Kingdom had the godly king, Jehoshaphat, he had formed an alliance with ungodly Ahab. His son had taken the daughter of Ahab and Jezebel in marriage (probably to seal the alliance). This girl, Athaliah, was a true disciple of her mother, so that by the time she herself was a grandmother, she came within a hair of wiping out the royal Davidic line (II Chronicles 21:5-7; 22:1-4,10-12).[48]

No wonder then that Jehovah miraculously intervened at Mount Carmel to remind the people once again that He only was the living God of Israel. The dignified simplicity and grandeur with which Jehovah through Elijah exposed the futile frenzies of eight hundred and fifty false prophets is a story which never loses its thrill even after numerous retellings. Although the apostate worship of Jeroboam's calf continued until it was wiped out in judgment, the back of Baal worship was effectively broken by Elijah's confrontation with the false prophets of Israel. In spite of later clandestine manifestations, Baal worship never again approached the status of an official religion.

For God to complete His purposes, the world must know that He spoke through Israel. His signs and wonders on their behalf attest that He did.

After the death of Elisha, Elijah's successor, miracles became rare in Israel until the coming of Christ. It is never the Lord's method to multiply wonders for the mere entertainment, gratification, or astonishment of mankind. They were His attention-getters, flashing the signal that said: "I am God, listen to My messenger and heed My message."

It remained for God's greatest Spokesman — the One for whom all earlier spokesmen waited — to be attested by His greatest miracles. The ministry of Christ was accompanied by such a display of omnipotence as has never been seen. He was miraculously conceived and born of a virgin. His identity was established by miracles. His great act of redemption, the crucifixion, was certified by the miracle of the resurrection.

The credentials of His apostles and the supernatural character of His church were established by the miracle of Pentecost. The status of the church as a worldwide organism, open to Gentile as well as to Jew, is conclusively proclaimed after the miraculous conversion of Paul and the signs that accompanied his work. B.B. Warfield has shown that supernatural manifestations in the church disappeared by the time the last persons on whom the apostles had personally laid hands were dead.[49] God by then had told us all we need to know. We can learn His mind by turning to the Word of God, the preserved messages of His accredited messengers.

The disciples on the day of Pentecost witnessed the enduement of the power of the Spirit of God with the accompanying visible miracles. But in his message, Peter made only a brief reference to the event. The miracle of tongues was a means to an end. Instead of dwelling on the miracle, Peter spoke about Christ and the miracles of His life, death, and resurrection. God began creating a new thing — His church, the body of Christ — through which to make His message of salvation known to all the world. That evangelistic teaching ministry began with the miracle of Pentecost.

With the death of the Apostle John, God's revelation was complete and the purpose and need for miracles was past. Late in his life John wrote the Holy Spirit's explanation for signs. John did not have space to record

PROPHECY: FORTHTELLING
OR FORETELLING?
Supernatural Evidence Continued

Elijah, when he preached against the evils of Baal worship, proved himself a spokesman for God by the miracles he performed. He was a prophet as well as a miracle-worker. He announced in advance that there would be no rain until he ordered it to resume. Before the rains did return, he predicted them to Ahab while the sky was still cloudless.

Prophecy and miracles are often hard to separate, but miracles chiefly point us to God as Creator (the God of nature), while prophecies call attention to the God who controls history — past, present and future. Before making their long-range statements, the great prophets presented their credentials by announcing short-range prophecies which their hearers could see fulfilled.

This was the very element in Christianity that led to the conversion of Justin Martyr, the great second-century apologist. He had gone the rounds of the numerous philosophies propounded by the best Greek schools of his day. But one day while walking by the seaside, he met a venerable man who pointed out to him how the life of Jesus Christ fulfilled the ancient Hebrew prophecies.

Convinced by further study, he became one of the outstanding defenders of the faith in the early church. In his testimony, he says concerning prophecy: "To delare a thing should come to pass long before it is in being and to bring it to pass, this or nothing is the work of God."

But our materialistic age seeks a natural explanation for everything unusual. Oswald T. Allis, in his introduction to the subject of prophecy, said: "Miracle and prophecy were formerly quite generally regarded by Christians as furnishing conspicuous, even irrefutable, proof of the truth and the divine authority of the Christian religion. They have now come to be regarded in many circles, even professedly Christian, as constituting the great and even insuperable obstacle to the acceptance of Biblical Christianity by the scientifically trained man and woman of today."[50] The same attitude that demands natural explanations for miracles seeks natural explanations for fulfilled prophecies — an effort to get rid of the supernatural. But, as Allis added, "To get rid of the supernatural in Christianity is to get rid of Christianity. For Christianity is supernatural in its very essence."[51]

THE PURPOSE OF PROPHECY

The result of such naturalism is that the great prophecies of Scripture are regarded as direct internal evidence that the passage must have been written after the event it foretells. If, as in many Messianic prophecies, it is impossible to date the text as late as the fulfillment took place, then either later editors are alleged to have altered the text, or the whole is reinterpreted — often by convenient changes in the text or by suggesting that originally it referred to some event parallel to the fulfillment.

For example, in Psalm 2:11,12, we read, "Serve the Lord with fear, and rejoice with trembling, Kiss the son, lest he be angry." This is the natural translation. But the word for Son is "bar," an Aramaic word familiar in names like Simon bar-Jonah. Critics ask why one Aramaic word should appear in an old Hebrew Psalm. By assuming that its appearance in Hebrew is an editorial addition, they avoid the admitted theological implications of the natural reading. They alter the text to what they regard as a more acceptable reading. The word *bar* is placed several words earlier, an inconvenient conjunction (and) is eliminated, and a new translation achieved: "Serve the Lord with fear, with trembling kiss his feet, lest he be angry . . ." (so the RSV). Thus the Messianic implication is reduced to "a royal psalm composed for a coronation"[52] in ancient Israel which has in later times been "reinterpreted" and applied to "the ideal king of a future hoped-for restoration."

Not only is there no justification for altering the text by such linguistic gymnastics, but literature in the Ugaritic dialect, which closely resembles Hebrew and was written before 1200 B.C., also contains such Aramaisms. Thus there is evidence against the assumption on which the alteration was made.

God knew that when the children of Israel entered Canaan their greatest temptation would be, not the moral sins of the list forbidden in the Decalogue, but the worship of the gods of the Canaanites.

Way back in the time of Moses, God promised to guide His people through His prophets. Israel was encamped near Mount Nebo on the eve of their entry into the Promised Land after a forty-year delay. Moses knew that soon he would climb that mountain alone to die and another would lead his flock into the land. Except for Joshua and Caleb, all those about to enter were the children and grandchildren of the Hebrews who had left Egypt. Would they remember what Moses had taught with such difficulty? Would they trust God though their parents had not? In four great discourses (which comprise the book of Deuteronomy, or second giving of the Law),

Moses reminds Israel of their deliverance, their covenant with Jehovah, and their duties in their new homeland. Among other things he tells them how to know God's will after God takes him from their midst.

Deuteronomy 18:9-11 specifically names some of the pagan Canaanite practices that were forbidden to Israel. Some of these may be unthinkable to our civilization — as passing our sons through fire, but astrology is not so unfamiliar. It may be understood as the meaning of the phrase "an observer of times" (verse 10). Spiritism (mediums and witchcraft), which we understand to be meant by the warnings against dealing with those that have familiar spirits or with necromancers, has today become a thriving business. These latter prohibitions demonstrate that man today is not much different from the ancients in his desire to know the future.

Ancient astrology was much like that of today, a belief that stars and planets — especially the signs of the zodiac — influence human acts and destinies so that by knowing their meanings and the relation of an individual to them, his life could be read. In many Oriental countries much of life is ruled today by astrologers. The horoscope pages of our newspapers show that it is common in the West. Hitler in his last days is said to have paid attention to his astrologer. You may have a neighbor who will not take a plane ride or invest in a business unless his horoscope is favorable. The Israelites were not to order their lives by any kind of fortune-teller. They had no need for these unreliable seers. God promised not to leave them without guidance.

The ability to predict the future has always been regarded as a sign of contact with the supernatural powers. If a man could only find out God's plans, then he could get in step with them. This opportunity God has given us in revealing His plan for the ages. And He taught us how to differentiate between His prophets and dabblers in the occult.

After forbidding all the ways of foretelling the future that the heathen practiced, God through Moses made the gracious promise that He did not intend to leave His people groping in the dark without guidance. Someday He would raise up a Prophet like unto Moses. This we understand to refer to Christ. In the meantime, until the ultimate fulfillment of this promise, some would be given the gift of prophecy. How would they be recognized? "When a prophet speaketh in the name of the Lord, if the thing follow not, nor come to pass, that is the thing which the Lord hath not spoken, but the prophet hath spoken it presumptuously; thou shalt not be afraid of him" (verse 22).

Isaiah, the "Prince of Prophets," had such a vision of the Lord that he gave himself wholly to do God's will in the year King Uzziah died. Isaiah tried to bring the wicked King Ahaz to obedient trust; Isaiah assisted good King Hezekiah in the great revival that marked his reign. His prophecies consisted of both the short-ranged predictions which could be known only to God and were intended to impress his hearers, and also long-range ones. An example of the first category is found in connection with his futile effort to bring the wicked king Ahaz into obedient trust (Isaiah 7). He then promised that within the short span of only two or three years, both the king's adversaries would lose their thrones. It came to pass.

Again, in the days of the good king Hezekiah, when Jerusalem was surrounded and the situation seemed hopeless, Isaiah not only promised relief, but also that Sennacherib, the Assyrian king, would "hear a rumor, and shall return to his own land" where he would "fall by the sword in his own land" (II Kings 19:7). How could Isaiah have known? Yet, not only was the siege lifted as prophesied, but we have an Assyrian inscription which confirms that the king was murdered after he returned.[53]

Isaiah, under the Spirit's control, reached nearly a century into the future when he prophesied Judah's captivity by Babylon — God's judgment on her backsliding. He reached ahead almost two centuries when he said that the captivity would end and Judah would be restored to her land when King Cyrus (of the then unknown land called Persia) made it possible. His prophecy swept on nearly eight centuries to predict that a virgin would conceive and bear a Son. He said that Son would preach good tidings to the meek and be led as a lamb to the slaughter, but His days would be prolonged. Then, piercing the curtain of century after century until they became millennia, he foretold that the governments of the world would be placed upon the shoulders of this Son. Which of these prophecies was too hard for God to fulfill or to foresee?

Some modern theologians would tell us that all of them are. Because some make God in their own image and cut Him down to finite proportions, they stagger in unbelief at prophecy. Isaiah, they suggest, was an astute observer of political and foreign affairs and so he saw the ascendancy of Babylon and the captivity of Judah. But as for his accurate prophecy concerning Cyrus, they maintain that a "second Isaiah" of equal astuteness wrote this prediction a century or more after the first Isaiah. The second Isaiah, the "great unknown" as some call him, did not write of a suffering Messiah, but according to the modern theological interpretation, he was referring to the sufferings of Israel in Isaiah 53. And the millennial kingdom — that is a beautiful, recurring Jewish dream! God's promise to Israel was that He would raise up another prophet like Moses who would teach them all they must know. That prophet was Christ, who when He came delivered God's *last* Word (Acts 3:20-26; Hebrews 1:1-3). This is why God does not speak today as He did in the past. We have His revelation complete and available for consultation in every need (Deuteronomy 29:29; II Timothy 3:16,17).

We know we have His complete and accurate revelation

the same way Israel knew they had His Word. We can test Israel's spokesmen by the short-range prophecies their contemporaries saw fulfilled, and by the long-range prophecies they had to accept by faith but now are history. They have been fulfilled. Thus prophecy is for us another evidence — a basic one — of the infallibility of God's Scripture and the truth of our faith. We can safely rest our souls, as did Justin Martyr, on the certainty of those prophecies as yet unfulfilled, knowing that the same God who put the fulfilled ones in the mouths of His spokesmen, put the still future ones there also.

Until God's perfect and final Prophet appeared, God from time to time sent spokesmen, and Israel need not worry about discerning the true from the false. God verified His prophets by the fact that their prophecies came true. Both true and false prophets sought to be heard, but God always vindicated His own. You may enjoy reviewing the contest of Micaiah with the false prophets of Ahab in II Chronicles 18, or of Jeremiah's vindication against the false Hananiah told in Jeremiah 28, as two examples.

Another interesting case of long-range prophecy fulfilled within the time of the Old Testament is that of the unknown prophet who appeared at the altar of Bethel on the occasion of its dedication. Jeroboam, Solomon's servant, was made king over the ten northern tribes of Israel in fulfillment of God's prophecy (I Kings 11:26-40). This left one tribe, Judah, over which Rehoboam, Solomon's son, reigned. (The tribe of Benjamin is usually included with Judah, as in I Kings 12:21). Jeroboam had the tribes as God had promised, but he began to worry that by going down to Jerusalem to worship, his subjects would be weaned back to the Davidic monarchy. To counteract this possible tendency he erected at Bethel a center of worship which featured a golden calf as the steed on which the invisible Jehovah sat. Most of the people made no distinction in their worship. They worshiped the calf instead of Jehovah.

Jehovah Himself interrupted the dedication of this altar by sending a prophet to foretell its destruction and even name the man who would be responsible for it.

Nearly three hundred years passed. The nation Jeroboam founded — the northern Kingdom of Israel — sank further and further into idolatry and finally was taken into captivity by the Assyrians. In the southern kingdom of Judah a young reformer of the Davidic line — Josiah by name — came to the throne and so thoroughly performed his job that he carried his reforms into the territory of the now desolate and scattered northern people. After doing a thorough job of eliminating the infamous shrine at Bethel, he found the grave of an unknown prophet and asked questions concerning him. Only then did he learn that he himself was the fulfillment of prophecy (II Kings 23:15-18).

The critics of prophecy have lost their vision both of God's omniscience and His purpose in prophesying. The prophets, they say, were preachers — forthtellers of God's will as they understood it. They spoke to their contemporaries in light of the needs and problems of their own day. If they made an astute prediction it was owing to the fact that they were more observant than the average good students of the contemporary scene, and farsighted in their understanding. If they did any foretelling, it was incidental and unimportant to their message.

THE GOD OF PROPHECY

But why should not the messenger of God be a foreteller? Knowing the attacks against Isaiah which would come in the latter days, God imbedded at the beginning of the section that would be attributed to the make-believe second Isaiah some challenging questions of Isaiah 41:21-29. He demands of the heathen idols, "Show the former things . . . or declare us things for to come!"

The God who could reveal the former things (Genesis) could declare the remote future (Revelation). Just to prove it, He looked a couple centuries ahead and pointed out Cyrus.

Yet this remarkable Cyrus prophecy has become in the hands of critics the cornerstone of the argument that Isaiah 40-66 was not written by the great prophet of Hezekiah's time but by some unknown who toward the end of the Babylonian exile surveyed the scene with remarkable insight and picked a contemporary king as God's servant who would punish "Babylon who art to be destroyed" (Psalm 137:8).

They use three arguments for change of authorship. First is *change of style*, forgetting that change of subject may change one's style and that one's style matures with time. Furthermore, the prophecy which God gave Hezekiah — that his sons should be carried into captivity in Babylon (Isaiah 39:7) — appears as a fitting setting into which to introduce the passage of consolation and hope which would mean so much to the captives who would fulfill the prophecy made to Hezekiah. For them Isaiah develops his exalted description of God.

The second argument against Isaianic authorship is the *theological content* of the chapters — the exalted concept of God which the critics consider a late development. This brings us back to rejecting again, as we did in an earlier study, the current theory of the evolution of religious ideas. The concepts of revelation and of evolution are not compatible. There is no reason to believe that the theological ideas of Isaiah 40—66 could not have been understood in the time of Hezekiah.

The third support of the argument against Isaianic authorship refers to the *historical allusions* of the later chapters which could not so clearly depict the conditions of the exile, the critics say, unless the author was contemporary with the events. It is a humanistic approach that denies the possibility of a revelation of the well in each individual. In a whole world that had sold out to evil, He could see and pick out the one righteous man, Noah. He took note of and commended the life of Job, condescending even to give him a personal answer to his questions. As we have seen, He called Josiah and Cyrus by name long before they lived. Daniel was known personally to Jehovah and was "a man greatly beloved" (Daniel 10:11).

Over and over, in both Testaments, He has demonstrated His awareness of individuals: to Nathaniel, Jesus said, "Before that Philip called thee, when thou wast under the fig tree, I saw thee" (John 1:48). He showed His careful planning on behalf of individuals: when He sent Ananias to Saul it was with the introduction, "he is a chosen vessel unto me" (Acts 9:15). He showed His concern even for those who did not know Him: concerning the shipmates of Paul, He promised, "God hath given thee all them that sail with thee" (Acts 27:24). To all men He has gone on record as "not willing that any should perish" (II Peter 3:9). With the psalmist we may be assured, "Thou knowest my downsitting and mine uprising, thou understandest my thought afar off" (Psalm 139:2).

We live in a world tortured by fear and beset with anxiety. Men's hearts are failing them for fear, perhaps a forerunner of that day yet future described by our Lord in Luke 21:26. God's prophecies are the secret of Christian serenity in these days. Only Christians know for sure what the future holds — that "freedom from want and freedom from fear" are going to be realities and that men's age-long dreams of peace and security will come true. Best of all, we know the One who holds the future and we rest safely in His hands.

The God who knows the past knows our past and has made provision to forgive it; He who knows the future knows our future and will use it for His glory and our best interest (Romans 8:28,29).

instrument in the return.

How did Isaiah, living one hundred fifty years before it happened, and using the Hebrew language, know anything about the given name (in the Persian language) of an as-yet-undreamed-of king? The liberals cannot understand nor explain that fact so they conclude some later person's writings became attached to his work.

Of course, Isaiah also told about both the first and second comings of Christ — prophecies far more long range than those concerning Cyrus.

What is, after all, the difference between history and prophecy but the place where we are standing? Should you be asked whether Chicago is east or west, your answer will depend on whether you are in Philadelphia or Denver. Time, space, and direction are all dependent on a point of view. Revelation gives us God's point of view.

We may liken God's point of view to that of a camera in a space ship. Its lens can take a view of earth which covers territory requiring a couple of days to travel by car or weeks by covered wagon. Should a lens be developed powerful enough to pick out details on these vast geographical stretches, it would show a Texas housewife taking her midmorning coffee break at the same instant that a man in Los Angeles is rushing for an early commuter train. What we see as past, present, and future is all as one to the God "that sitteth on the circle of the earth" (Isaiah 40:22).

The most wonderful part of all this is that God has been pleased to share His plans with us. He could have left us groping blindly, wondering what was the end and purpose of life. But because He cared enough to redeem us from the slavery of sin into which we had sold ourselves, He cared enough also to show us what He had in store.

More than all this it is wonderful to know that this same God, who has in His hands the great sweep of history and the rise and fall of nations, is interested as well in each individual. In a whole world that had sold out to evil, He could see and pick out the one righteous man, Noah. He took note of and commended the life of Job, condescending even to give him a personal answer to his questions. As we have seen, He called Josiah and Cyrus by name long before they lived. Daniel was known personally to Jehovah and was "a man greatly beloved" (Daniel 10:11).

Over and over, in both Testaments, He has demonstrated His awareness of individuals: to Nathaniel, Jesus said, "Before that Philip called thee, when thou wast under the fig tree, I saw thee" (John 1:48). He showed His careful planning on behalf of individuals: when He sent Ananias to Saul it was with the introduction, "he is a chosen vessel unto me" (Acts 9:15). He showed His concern even for those who did not know Him: concerning the shipmates of Paul, He promised, "God hath given thee all them that sail with thee" (Acts 27:24). To all men He has gone on record as "not willing that any should perish" (II Peter 3:9). With the psalmist we may be assured, "Thou knowest my downsitting and mine uprising, thou understandest my thought afar off" (Psalm 139:2).

We live in a world tortured by fear and beset with anxiety. Men's hearts are failing them for fear, perhaps a forerunner of that day yet future described by our Lord in Luke 21:26. God's prophecies are the secret of Christian serenity in these days. Only Christians know for sure what the future holds — that "freedom from want and freedom from fear" are going to be realities and that men's age-long dreams of peace and security will come true. Best of all, we know the One who holds the future and we rest safely in His hands.

The God who knows the past knows our past and has made provision to forgive it; He who knows the future knows our future and will use it for His glory and our best interest (Romans 8:28,29).

MISSING MONARCHS
Evidence from History

The Book of Daniel shares with the Pentateuch and the second half of Isaiah the dubious distinction of being singled out for special concentrated attack by those who spend their careers eliminating everything supernatural from the Bible. So vicious have been the attacks that at the turn of the century Sir Robert Anderson wrote a defense of the book which he entitled, *Daniel in the Critics' Den.* It is safe to say that the lions treated the prophet with far more respect than have his modern theological enemies.

It is, of course, the large element of prophecy in the writing which they call in question; but because their method of attacking the prophecy is to attack the credibility of the historical portions of the work, it is part of the work of Christian Evidences to establish the historicity of the book.

A few decades ago, a remarkable ancient document was discovered. It was the Persian King Cyrus' own account of how he captured Babylon. By his description, it was a pushover. "When I made my triumphal entrance into Babylon with joy and rejoicing I took up my lordly residence in the royal palace." After attributing the easy victory to Marduk (the Bel of Isaiah 46:1-13) and claiming to restore his temples which had fallen into ruins, he adds, "My numerous troops marched peacefully into Babylon."[54] Apparently a welcoming committee was there to greet him.

Many critics were not surprised to find that this document made no mention of Belshazzar. After all, neither Herodotus nor Xenophon (ancient Greek historians) mention him either, although they do discuss the fall of Babylon. Thus it seemed once again that the remarkable story of Belshazzar's feast in Daniel 5 might prove to be the fancy of some ill-informed late writer. As Boutflower has said, "Critics look upon the Book of Daniel as a religious novel . . . written about 164 B.C."[55]

SOME LOST MONARCHS FOUND

We shall probably better understand the importance of history's corroboration of the book of Daniel if we first look at the classic critical approach to it, much as we did at the documentary theory of the Pentateuch.

If the young man named Daniel, who was carried into Babylon in the third year of the reign of Jehoiakim a few years before the final deportation from Judah to Babylon, is the same one who became the advisor of Babylonian kings, and if he was also the author of the book of Daniel (which it claims for itself), then the book was written in the sixth century B.C. However, the prophetic chapters in the work describe the fall of Babylon (539 B.C., Daniel 5:30; 8:1-4) and the rise of Persia, the conquest of Persia by Greece, the career of Alexander the Great from 336-322 B.C. (Daniel 8:5-7, 21,22; 11:3), and the rise of the Seleucid kings in Syria (8:8), especially the career of Antiochus Epiphanes from 175-163 B.C. (Daniel 11:21-35), in accurate detail.

It is because known history is so clearly fulfilled in this outline that the critics say Daniel was written about 167 B.C., the date when Antiochus desecrated the Temple in

Jerusalem. They maintain that it writes history leading up to that point as if it were written at the beginning rather than the end of an era. In the words of a popular denominational adult Sunday School quarterly, Daniel is a book of history "surveyed as if it were being predicted." Actually, there is nothing "modern" about this false view. About A.D. 300 an anti-Christian philosopher named Porphyry first made the suggestion that Daniel must have been written after the reign of Antiochus Epiphanes. Such reasoning is, of course, really a compliment to Daniel's prophetic accuracy. For us, the basic proof of authorship is the fact that our Lord ascribed it to the prophet Daniel (see Matthew 24:15; Mark 13:14).

So wedded are the critics to their second-century date that even after the finding of the Dead Sea Scrolls, they still cling to the theory. Among the scrolls was found a fragment of the second chapter of the book of Daniel, which contained the transition from Hebrew to Aramaic in Daniel 2:4. The critics will not forsake their theory despite the complication that it does not allow enough time needed for the steps required by their explanations. So difficult is it to accept the supernatural when one's whole outlook is against it, that Professor G.R. Driver (who wrote the introduction to the Old Testament of the New English Bible) argued for a later date to be accepted for the Dead Sea fragments (in spite of all the evidence that they must be early) because an earlier date would have to be assigned to the original writing of Daniel![56]

Believers are now in the happy situation of living in a day when some of the jaws of the critical lions have been stopped by the uncovering of new historical evidence. In the past they "proved" Daniel to be a second-century writer who knew nothing about events which took place in the sixth century because he "invented" a king of Babylon named Belshazzar who was completely unknown to history. Today they admit the second-century author must have had some sixth-century source material.

Although the critics have accused the book of Daniel of errors in nearly every chapter, perhaps the dramatic story of Belshazzar has been the object of more than its share. After all, it involves all the objectional factors — from the miraculous to fulfilled prophecy — which make it incredible and even obnoxious to those who would rule the supernatural out of their theology.

In this incident we see first of all the king who should be mending his fences and preparing for invasion, feasting and carousing. Second, he goes out of his way to insult the God of the Hebrews, who dwell in his kingdom, by calling for vessels confiscated from their temple and desecrating them to indulge his lusts and worship his pagan gods.

Then comes the miracle — the disembodied hand that writes for all to see. In a land noted for its astrologers and soothsayers, none could or would read this writing although apparently it was in Aramaic, the trade language of the age.

Just at this point of dismay, the queen appears and reminds the king of an aged, respected advisor from his father's court, who had on former occasions interpreted dreams. Perhaps he should be called. When Daniel arrives, sensing the end of Belshazzar and his kingdom is near, he rejects the soon-to-be-useless gifts, reads the cryptic words and explains that they are a prophetic warning from God. Belshazzar's kingdom has been judged and delivered to his adversaries. The record concludes: "In that night was Belshazzar the king of the Chaldeans slain. And Darius the Median took the kingdom. . ." (Daniel 5:30,31).

They were right as far as Belshazzar's being unknown is concerned. Available historical records at the time showed that the last Babylonian king was Nabonidus, and that far from being killed the night the Medes and

Persians captured the city, he was far away in the Arabian town of Tema.

Again, the sands of time have yielded up the answer. First, tablets were discovered containing the name of Belshazzar, showing that there really was such a person, after all. Then a tablet came to light that linked the names of Belshazzar and Nabonidus, and at last one that showed Belshazzar to be King Nabonidus' firstborn son. Still unbelief clung to the fact that Nabonidus was the last king of Babylon and did not die in the fall of the city but, rather, was pensioned off by the conquering Persians. Eventually a tablet was unearthed which read, "He entrusted a camp to his eldest, firstborn son; the troops of the land went with him. He freed his hand; he entrusted the kingship to him, then he himself undertook a distant campaign . . . ."[57] The Nabonidus chronicle records that in the seventh, ninth, tenth, and eleventh years of the king, Nabonidus was in Tema, and "the son of the king . . . in the land of Akkad" (Babylonia). More and more business documents are being discovered which show that the scribes dated to both Nabonidus and Belshazzar. There now remains no doubt that Belshazzar was co-monarch with his father and was in the city of Babylon when Cyrus captured it.

This explains one odd little item in the story — why the king offered third, not second, place (Daniel 5:7) to the interpreter. This, in a remarkable way, though an inconspicuous detail, receives corroboration. Daniel is shown to be a chronicler of history who knew some of its small footnotes not available to a writer who lived three centuries after him.

Neither should the record be criticized (as it has) for calling Belshazzar a son of Nebuchadnezzar, when actually Nabonidus was his father. Nabonidus was apparently the son of a favorite concubine of Nebuchadnezzar (born to another man before she joined the royal harem), and there is reason to believe that the queen, Belshazzar's mother, was Nicotris, a daughter of Nebuchadnezzar. It is not at all uncommon for the term *father* to be applied to one's ancestors. There is evidence that later monarchs referred to their predecessors in such a term even where no blood relationship existed.

Belshazzar is not the only instance of a lost Biblical monarch being restored to his place in history. Sargon, king of Assyria from 722-705 B.C., also disappeared from history. A.T. Olmstead, in his *History of Assyria*, tells of the modern peasants of the village of Khorsabad picking their way among the rubble of ancient bricks inscribed with the name of Sargon. "But for long ages," he continues, "none could read the writing, and the only proof of his existence was due to the accidental fact that a prophet in a petty western kingdom happened to have dated a sermon by the year when his Turanu (Tartan, or general) took Ashdod (Isaiah 20:1). So little did this establish his identity, such is the irony of fate, that scholars long argued that he was the same as that Shalmaneser [V] whose throne he had usurped."[58] Others proposed the name of Sennacherib, his son, on the assumption that the text was corrupt.

With the discovery of more and more ancient evidences, we know now that this Sargon was one of the great conqueror-kings of Assyria, extremely important in his day. In fact, we have his own detailed account of this expedition to Ashdod mentioned in Isaiah, which dates to 711 B.C. Even the strange act of the prophet — to prefigure the judgment of Ashdod by going naked for three years — has been substantiated by engraved ivory found at Megiddo depicting naked captives dragged by ropes around their necks before their conqueror. As Olmstead says in another place, "The monuments have corrected the critics, and have given us a full account of this very campaign (against Ashdod), but the heading (verse 1) of Isaiah 20 has corrected the monuments, by proving that the leader of the expedition was the Turanu official and not the king."[59]

Another forgotten monarch to turn up in the monuments is Pharaoh Shishak of Egypt. He apparently not only received tribute from Rehoboam (II Chronicles 12), but went into the northern kingdom of Israel. Though not mentioned in the Old Testament, we learn this from a stela he erected at Megiddo.

Robert Dick Wilson made an interesting study of the accuracy of the transmission of the names of Old Testament kings. As a result, he says: "Thus we find that in 143 cases of transliteration from Egyptian, Assyrian, Babylonian and Moabite into Hebrew and in 40 cases of the opposite, or 184 in all, the evidence shows that for 2300 to 3900 years the text of the proper names of the Hebrew Bible has been transmitted with the most minute accuracy. That the original scribes should have written them with such close conformity to correct philological principles is a wonderful proof of their thorough care and scholarship; further, that the Hebrew text should have been transmitted by copyists through so many centuries is a phenomenon unequaled in the history of literature."[60]

Then, just in case the reader might think it not unusual for historians to be accurate in these matters, Wilson turns to the ancient secular historians, Manetho, Ptolemy, and Pseudo-Callisthenes to demonstrate how frequently we are unable to identify transmitted names, and adds: "The late President Woolsey of Yale College has truly said, that in the Greek manuscripts and in the versions 'proper names assume different forms at will.' Thus we see not merely analogical evidence but the direct evidence of the documents forces us to the conclusion that the spelling of the proper names of the kings as given in the Old Testament must go back to original sources; and if the original sources were in the hands of the composers of the documents, the probability is that since the composers are correct in the spelling of the names of the kings they are correct also in the sayings and deeds which they record concerning these kings."[61]

NOT ALL ARE FOUND

Lest the impression be given that new historical evidence has given us all the answers, it must be said there is much yet to learn. We can expect at best only to "know in part." Much remains for the area of faith in the authority of the Author of the statements.

The critics have been stopped on the matter of Belshazzar, but they did not have to go far in order to carry on. In the last two verses of the same chapter was the mysterious king, "Darius the Mede." There seems to be as little room for him in the historical chronology as there once appeared to be for Belshazzar. Both Herodotus and Xenophon, the Greek historians, tell us that Babylon was conquered by Cyrus, King of Persia. They corroborate many details of the Scripture; for example, that Babylon was taken unaware by a ruse, as prophesied in Jeremiah 50:24. They record that the Median and Persian armies dug trenches that diverted the course of the Euphrates and made it possible for them to walk in under the walls by way of the river bed. The expression "make the crooked places straight" (Isaiah 45:2) seems to refer to the rechanneling of the Euphrates in the time of Cyrus.

These historians also report that there was a great revelry in progress at the time so that the leaders were unaware that the city was being taken until the conquerors burst in upon them. However, they, like the Cyrus cylinder quoted above, have nothing to say about a Darius becoming king of Babylon. Although a more accurate translation of Daniel 5:31 is that Darius "received" the kingdom the critics ignore the marvelous fulfillment of Jeremiah's prophecy (Daniel 9:1,2; cf. Jeremiah 25:12; 29:10) and the corroboration of the historians and grasp to their bosoms this argument from silence.

The classical critical view thus concludes that Darius was the fictitious invention of the Daniel who supposedly wrote the book in the second century B.C. and who wrote immediate past history as if it were prophecy. Daniel 9:1, however, makes clear that Darius was not a natural but an appointed king, no doubt by Cyrus himself (Daniel 6:28).

Cyrus did have a general Gubaru whom he appointed over affairs at Babylon, and some identify him as Darius the Mede. Professor John Whitcomb has written an extended discussion of this, in which he concludes: "It is true that the name Darius the Mede has not yet been found in any extra-Biblical inscription of pre-Christian times. Nevertheless, Gubaru the Governor of Babylon fits the Biblical description of Darius the Mede so remarkably that the writer believes he will be recognized in due time as the monarch who played such an important role in the life of Daniel after the Fall of Babylon."[62]

Josephus, when he mentions Darius the Mede, remarks that he was known by another name among the Greeks — what name evidently escaped his memory. It is also true that no inscriptions have been uncovered which suggest that Gubaru was ever called Darius. Thus he remains an enigma. Whether he is Gubaru or some other person as yet unknown to the historians awaits future confirmation. And we may be sure when the time comes he will be recognized to be as real as Belshazzar has proven to be.

Similarly, there have been unsuccessful attempts to identify the kings of Genesis 14. For a time it seemed that Amraphel could be equated with the famous lawgiver Hammurabi, mentioned in Chapter 3. But this identification has been discarded since the best dating for Abraham now seems to suggest that he must have lived about two hundred years before Hammurabi. Perhaps in time documents or monuments will be uncovered that will shed light on this mysterious episode and the nine kings who participated in it.

The mere fact that we are ignorant of sources outside the Bible, pertaining to some particular ancient monarch or incident, does not mean that we are dealing with fiction. In the first place, those who do not accept the Bible as God's Word are revealing their bias against it when they do not at least accept it as a very ancient document on an equal footing with other ancient documents which claim to be history.

But even aside from that, enough Biblical history has been found to be in agreement with other ancient sources to have earned the confidence of the open-minded for the whole. And nothing has been found which is in flat contradiction to it. There is no reason why we should not expect further corroborative material to be discovered from time to time. We would do well to learn a lesson from the blind man whose sight was restored by Jesus, as recorded for us in John 9:6,7. He did not see who had healed him, but when he was called upon to make an identification, he could reply fearlessly and confidently, "One thing I know, that, whereas I was blind, now I see" (John 9:25). This was the one all-encompassing fact in the man's life. The Man who had given him vision was worthy of his utmost trust; with this assurance he dared instruct even the Pharisees (verses 29-34).

We may not know all the relevant facts of Bible history, and we may not have all the information necessary to refute the criticisms of those who are better at tearing down than at building. We do know, however, that this Book has brought us from darkness to light, and that the Author of this Book is the Light of the world who has shined in our hearts. The Author and the Book which have given us spiritual vision can be trusted. Our faith is well-grounded. We may never have all the historical answers, but their lack does not alter the revealed truth. Now we know in part, and in the face of this partial knowledge we still have abiding faith and hope and love (I Corinthians 13:12,13).

THE JESUS OF HISTORY
Evidence for an Accurate Biblical Text

Albert Schweitzer, who became famous in three different careers — that of musician, of theologian, and of medical missionary — and ended his life almost officially sainted by the liberal wing of Protestantism, counted among his early achievements a book entitled *The Quest for the Historical Jesus.* In this work he sought to strip the gospel story of all "legendary" additions, specifically anything supernatural, and to find the "real Jesus behind the myths." His book was acclaimed and widely quoted.

What do we know about the *real* historical Jesus? This favorite discussion of liberal theologians is reflected in much popular religious writing. While it is no longer fashionable to doubt the actual existence of a person called Jesus of Nazareth by suggesting He was the figment of His disciples' imagination since He left no writing of His own, these theologians still cannot admit that we have any reliable historical information concerning Him. One popular history text flatly states, "Because we have no precise, contemporary accounts, the exact details of the preachings of Jesus during his own lifetime cannot always be determined."[63] To the writer of this history, it is only the "general nature of his message" that is clear.

The attitude quoted above is not uncommon in the

textbooks and there is much talk of "demythologizing" Jesus, or of getting back of the Gospels to the "real Jesus." Such efforts are not new. Thomas Jefferson attempted to reveal the "pure principles" of Christianity by returning to "the very words only of Jesus." He desired to "strip off the artificial vestments in which they have been muffled by priests." Jefferson thus proceeded to expunge "everything that failed to satisfy his own reason, presenting Jesus solely as a human being and teacher of morals." Somehow he felt he could write on the title page of the resulting work: this book "is a document in proof that I am a *real* Christian."[64]

HOW DO WE KNOW ABOUT CHRIST?

The popularity of red-letter editions of the New Testament may be partly due to a general subconscious feeling that somehow the words of Jesus are more sacred or more reliable than the rest of the New Testament. The fact is overlooked that the words of Jesus are found in the same Gospels that describe His miracles. If the other portions of the Gospels are not reliable, we have no assurance that Christ's words are recorded correctly. Either we take the whole record at face value or we are open to the charge of reading into it what we choose to see and not what it actually says.

However, in the nineteenth century, the Tubingen School (named for the University of Tubingen, Germany) using its anti-supernatural bias, developed a widely accepted theory that most of the New Testament books were written in the middle of the second century A.D. and represented a late development of church doctrine. Only four of Paul's epistles (Romans, I and II Corinthians, and Galatians) were admitted to date from the first century when Paul lived. All the documents on which we depend for the life of Christ and the development of the church were included by the Tubingen School among those dated late. Thus the

Gospels and Acts would become unreliable as historical sources.

Although much subsequent textual study and archaeological discoveries have proved the Tubingen thesis to be without a historical leg on which to stand, its theories still crop up in popular writings. Actually, the text of our New Testament is better attested than any other of the great historical writings which have come down to us from the Greek and Roman eras. Despite documentation many people carefully avoid facing the issues by hiding behind some supposed doubt about the authenticity of the gospel story. There is abundant evidence of accuracy and reliability of the Christian message as we have it today, and every Christian ought to know something about the mass of evidence which confirms his faith.

According to the rules of historical evidence, the best reporter of any event is an eyewitness to that event, and when the testimony of several eyewitnesses is in substantial agreement, the historicity of the event cannot be reasonably doubted.

To whom do we owe the Gospel accounts of the life of Christ? Let us look first at the little postscript at the end of John's Gospel (21:24,25), which seems to be attached as a witness or kind of notary. This more assures the reader that the writer of the book is indeed the Apostle John who was with Jesus during His ministry and experienced personally that of which he wrote. In I John 1:1, the apostle confirms that he was an eyewitness. He begins his letter by emphasizing that he has actually *seen*, *heard*, and *handled*.

Peter, too (II Peter 1:16-18), is careful to tell his readers that his teaching is that of an eyewitness who is writing about what he has seen. The testimony of the earliest church fathers is that Mark's Gospel was written under the direct supervision of Peter and accepted by the church as Peter's Gospel.

Matthew, too, qualifies as an eyewitness since he was

one of the twelve apostles.

Luke probably was not an eyewitness of our Lord's earthly ministry but says in his introduction (Luke 1:1-4) that he collected his material from those who were. His record is not hearsay. Furthermore, he worked closely with Paul.

The late Sir William Ramsey was responsible for the first serious challenges to the theories of the Tubingen School. Trained as a Greek scholar, he was a convinced follower of that school and of the Wellhausen Hypothesis. According to his own testimony "I began then to study Acts in search of geographical and antiquarian evidence, hardly expecting to find any but convinced that if there were any, it would bear on the condition of Asia Minor in the time the writer lived."[65]

He then followed the journeys of Paul and returned home satisfied that the archaeological evidence he had discovered proved a first-century eyewitness must be the author — that Luke was a careful historian. Since Luke also wrote the Gospel bearing his name, Ramsey extended his studies until he brought down the whole methodology used by the Tubingen School.

The minute accuracy of the verifiable details in Luke's writings (Luke and Acts) have been subsequently so well demonstrated by disinterested and even antagonistic investigators that his reputation as a reliable historian is generally acknowledged.

Thus it is important to note that our accounts of the life of Christ purport to be the stories of the eyewitnesses themselves. A reading of the Scripture passages will confirm that many of them were careful to establish the fact that what they taught was what they themselves saw. In Acts 1:15-26, we have a record of the disciples' decision to elect to apostleship someone to fill the vacancy left by Judas. Their chief criterion for an acceptable candidate was that he must have been, like them, an eyewitness to the events of the ministry of Jesus and to His resurrection. Paul, too, stresses in defense of his apostleship that he also had seen the risen Lord (I Corinthians 15:8,9).

Despite these facts, some histories still talk of the New Testament books not completed until "late in the second or early in the third century."[66] F.F. Bruce notes, "A majority of modern scholars fix dates for the gospels" in the last third of the first century, easily within the life span of eyewitnesses. "But," he goes on to say, "good reasons have been given by Harnack and others for dating the first three gospels earlier."[67]

Conservatives generally accept that Luke was the latest of the three synoptic Gospels (Matthew, Mark, Luke) to be written: thus, if Luke's writings were intended as a defense for Paul at his first trial before Nero, as has been suggested, all three synoptics would have a date prior to A.D. 62. John is believed to have produced his writings during the last decade of the century.

Perhaps equally significant with the date of the original writings is the age of the oldest surviving copies and the number of copies that have survived. Altogether nearly five thousand Greek manuscripts have been found. But that is not the whole story. To quote F.F. Bruce again, "Perhaps we can appreciate how wealthy the New Testament is in manuscript attestation if we compare the textual material for other ancient historical works."[68]

He then continues by citing the extant manuscripts for Caesar, Livy, Tacitus, Thucydides, and Herodotus. If you took second year Latin, you probably read Caesar's *Gallic War* which was composed between 58 and 50 B.C. Of this there are only nine or ten good manuscripts, and the oldest is some 900 years later than Caesar. Of Tacitus (about A.D. 100) F.F. Bruce says, "The text of these extant portions of his two great historical works depends entirely on two MSS, one of the ninth century and one of the eleventh." Manuscripts for Thucydides and Herodotus are comparable. "Yet," Bruce concludes, "no classical scholar would listen to an argument that the authenticity of Herodotus or Thucydides is in doubt because the earliest MSS of their works which are of any use to us are over 1,300 years later than the originals."

With the manuscripts of the New Testament, the situation is vastly different. We have two excellent manuscripts of the fourth century and numerous fragments of from one to two hundred years earlier. We have some fragments of the four Gospels which date to A.D. 150, and one fragment containing John 18:31-33,37 which dates somewhere between A.D. 117 and 138, showing that the latest written Gospel (probably between A.D. 90 and 100) was circulating in Egypt within forty years of its writing.

In 1972, Father Jose O'Callaghan, a Spanish Jesuit Biblical scholar and papyrologist, made the astounding assertion that some fifteen Greek fragments found in one of the caves of the Dead Sea are fragments of I Timothy, Acts, James, Romans, II Peter and the Gospel of Mark. If these small fragments are supported by more evidence or are generally accepted, Father O'Callaghan's dating of the Mark fragment to A.D. 50 would give us evidence for the existence of the Gospel to within a quarter-century of the events it records.[69]

In addition to Greek manuscripts we also have fragments of early translations, especially Old Syriac and Old Latin, which date as far back as the second century — evidence enough that the originals had been well circulated before that date. Christians have always been people of the Book, and translations seem to have sprung up almost as fast as there was a group of Christians who read a given language.

A third evidence that the books of the New Testament were in circulation by the end of the first century comes from the numerous quotations in the writings of the early church fathers. The second century gave us many outstanding Christian apologists, some of which had known one or another of the apostles personally. The many quotations from the New Testament to be found in their works attest beyond question that the apostolic writings were in circulation and recognized as authoritative in their day.

To quote another manuscript authority, Sir Frederick Kenyon: "The interval then between the dates of original composition and the earliest extant evidence becomes so small as to be in fact negligible, and the last foundation for any doubt that the Scriptures have come down to us substantially as they were written has now been removed."[70]

These facts alone should make our Gospel accounts acceptable as authentic history. But, in addition, they have what no other history except the Old Testament can claim — the plenary inspiration of the Holy Spirit. Our Lord promised to ask the Father to send the Holy Spirit to abide with His disciples (John 14:16). He refers to Him as the Spirit of Truth who is unknown to the world, but known by believers. Of Him Christ says that He will dwell with the disciples and that He "shall be in you."

The Lord gives a little insight into the sphere of the Holy Spirit's ministry — He will indwell, He will teach, He will bring to mind things that have been learned. In other portions of Scripture we learn that the ministry of the Spirit of God included the infilling of the disciples to do the work entrusted to them and the moving of chosen godly men to accurately record His infallible authoritative Word.

Of course, if the Gospels are eyewitness history kept from error by the Holy Spirit, they cannot possibly be second-century forgeries. By the recognized rules of historical evidence our eyewitnesses to the life of Jesus should be accepted. But these writers have the added advantage of divine protection from faulty memory, careless misquotation, coloring for effect, or any other error which may mar the accuracy of a writer.

WHY DO WE TRUST THE TEXTS?

Although it has long been popular to suggest that from the wealth of early Christian writings certain books were selected and pronounced "canonical" (that is, the rule of standard of faith) by a church council, the fact is, the early church accepted our New Testament books as canonical from the time of their first appearance which was prior to the church council, and read them in their services as equal to the Old Testament. Why were just these — of all the early Christian writings — recognized as authoritative?

From the beginning, the church accepted as inspired Scripture only the writings of apostles or men closely associated with the apostles. Thus pains were taken to establish the genuineness of a work beyond doubt. Paul recognized this and in nearly all his epistles carefully guaranteed his authorship as can be seen in II Thessalonians 3:17 and every epistle written later. First Thessalonians 2:6,13 and I Timothy 4:1 show the writer recognized he was a special instrument of the Holy Spirit and his writings were to be classified as Scripture.

The early church produced an immense quantity of written material, much of it still well worth reading today. Yet the church never confused any of these writings — not even those which were most revered, copied, and read — as being on a par with the writings of our New Testament. Only those authoritative writings were accepted as Scripture, binding on the churches, and proper to read in the worship service. The apostles themselves recognized their work to be on a par with the Old Testament and recognized the same for each other's work (I Thessalonians 2:6,13; I Timothy 4:1; II Peter 3:15,16). With the death of the last apostle the canon of Scripture was closed forever, as intimated by Revelation 22:18,19. God had said all that was necessary and from then on would speak only through what was already written. The fact that it does still speak, that it has an answer for every problem, talks to all types and conditions of men, and is capable of endless reams of explanations without the depths of it being plumbed is sufficient evidence that these words are God's words and not man's.

Many so-called gospels of Jesus, sayings of Jesus, and the like, have come down to us, some of them popular among early Christians. But they were never equated with Scripture or read in the services. The four Gospels as we have them were from the earliest times the unanimously accepted authoritative accounts of His life.

The final objection to the historical reliability of the Gospels is voiced by those who call attention to variations among the copies which have come down to us. We do not, of course, have the original manuscripts (or "autographs") of the New Testament writers. We do know, however, that they were in existence as late as A.D. 200, because Tertullian, a church leader who lived about that time, wrote that the originals of the New Testament books could still be inspected in the churches founded by the apostles. The earliest copies were compared to these manuscripts, and we have portions that date earlier than Tertullian's time.

Among the thousands of copies that we do possess, there are admittedly many variations from one to another. For nearly fourteen hundred years, until the printing press was invented, all copies were made by hand.

A.D. 1453 is considered a turning point of history. The Fall of Constantinople is one reason, but Gutenberg's printing press (at about the same time) probably had more far-reaching influence. Before that time all books were copied laboriously by hand. Many monks spent their lives in perfecting copies of perhaps just one given portion of Scripture. Yet for all their loving care, the typical mistakes of copyists slowly crept into the text. Sometimes a scribe copied from an existing copy, and sometimes he listened and wrote as it was read to him. His ear or his eyes caught things inaccurately, or he inadvertently reversed two letters. At other times the reader's eye dropped too far and he would skip a line or a paragraph. He might incorporate into his text the marginal explanation of an earlier scribe. These were much the same as what we now call typographical errors. A mistake in spelling, doubling of a word, omission of a line, hearing a word wrong when the reader read to the scribe. Sometimes later copyists caught and corrected these errors on their copies, sometimes they were perpetuated. Here it is that the fascinating science of textual criticism comes to the Bible reader's aid.

Finding the Greek text of the New Testament is an exciting treasure hunt which has occupied the lifetime of many devoted scholars, with such success that we can safely say that our most up-to-date Greek New Testaments give us substantially the very words that were originally written.

The work of the textual critics is to study the New Testament manuscripts and fragments — almost 5,000 — to group them according to the types of differences, and to study them closely to ascertain which of several readings is the ancient one. By comparing one copy with another, and by tracing families of texts — that is, those which appear to have all come from a single source — textual critics have been able to ascertain in many cases which of these variants is correct.

In addition they compare the Greek texts with early copies of translations (Old Latin, Syriac, Coptic, Armenian, Ethiopic, Gothic, etc.) and with the quotations found in the writings of the church fathers. Thus they are able to decide what the reading was at the time of these writings. So thoroughly has their work been done we can be sure our best Greek text today is substantially that which was originally written. It is a relatively small part of the New Testament that has any question attaching to it. And these spots are well known and marked in our translations. If you have a Scofield Reference Bible you will find some of them carefully documented in the notes. The new revision of this Bible has expanded many of the notes to reflect the more recent manuscript findings.

Although the doctrine of plenary inspiration of the Scripture applies to the original writings, it can safely be maintained that the Holy Spirit has guided and superintended the preservation of His book throughout the centuries. No reliable scholar today can build a good case of lack of historicity in the contents of the writings or for corruption of the original documents of the writers.

As far as the life of Christ is concerned, the two major passages presently in question are the last twelve verses of Mark's Gospel and the story of the woman taken in adultery (John 7:53-8:11). Neither of these appears in the most ancient manuscripts. Yet, in the latter case at least, there is some evidence that there may be an omission in these rather than an addition in later manuscripts.

Our editions of the New Testament are trustworthy reproductions of the original writings. No other work of any of the ancient historians from the same Greek and Roman eras can be attested with nearly the same amount of accumulated evidence. The life of Christ as the Gospels give it to us in our English Bibles is the story of the real historic Jesus written by eyewitnesses and accurately transmitted to us. His sayings, His miracles, the meaning of His life, death and resurrection as recorded therein are all accurate. It is impossible to separate the Gospels into fact and legend. They must be accepted wholly as accurate history or the evidence must be ignored and the whole denied. The weight of testimony is in favor of the fact that "the Scripture cannot be broken" (John 10:35).

11

THE RESURRECTION
The Basic Christian Evidence

When a professor in a divinity school was asked whether he believed in the resurrection of Christ, he talked glibly about Christ's inspiring example, the revitalizing power of His teaching, and other such evasions. Pinned down to express himself as to the physical, bodily resurrection of Christ, he said, "If I had what seemed to be incontrovertible proof, I still would not believe it."

His problem was not with proofs but with pride, the same pride which made Thomas Jefferson paste together a personal Bible from which everything supernatural, including the resurrection, had been deleted. His admittedly vast scientific understanding could not fathom a physical resurrection, and his pride of intellect forced him to reject the possibility of something being a fact which did not square with his enlightened reason.

When theologians desert God's revelation for natural reason, they try to explain away and spiritualize the resurrection because it is an embarrassment to them. Such theologians seek to uplift society with an ethical and moral system palatable to the natural man. Historians, on the other hand, cannot so readily dismiss the fact of the resurrection. Examine practically any textbook of western civilization and you will find that, regardless of the personal faith of the writer, it will be stressed that the early Christians firmly believed Christ arose from the dead and that this is what welded them into a force that changed the world. Take that away and, whatever good is left, it is not the faith of the New Testament, the early church, or the great confessions.

Other great teachers have produced lofty ethical codes that have been accepted by large segments of society, but they have not produced the world-shaking dynamic of Christianity. Why? When Jesus was on earth He made some tremendous claims for Himself. He said He was the Son of God (John 10:30-38) and existed in eternity before His birth in Bethlehem (John 8:58). He said His death was voluntary; no man could kill Him (John 10:17,18). He said He had power to forgive sin (Mark 2:5-12). He said His suffering, death, and resurrection should be proclaimed to all mankind (Luke 24:44-48).

Normally, if a person made such claims we would say he was mad. Why do historians, even if they lack a personal faith in Jesus Christ take Him seriously? Why do we believe Him?

"WHOM HE HATH RAISED FROM THE DEAD"

The writings which told His story are reliable. We have an accurate record of what Jesus said and did. But to believe that His words are accurately reported is one thing; to believe He spoke truthfully when He said them is another. If the story of Jesus ended — as Thomas Jefferson's Bible made it end — with His burial, would we today believe all the claims He made for Himself?

Even the theologians most ready to call the New Testament documents pious second-century forgeries, admit the the epistles to the Corinthians are genuine works of Paul. And I Corinthians 15 is our great doctrinal passage concerning the resurrection. It may even have been written before the Gospels. In these verses Paul places the weight of his argument on the fact that the resurrection of Christ was a historically verifiable event. He names the people who can witness to it, and adds that at the time he was writing (about A.D. 55) most of them are still alive. Several of these eyewitnesses set down their testimonies and we can read them in their Gospels and epistles.

If you read through the book of Acts, pausing to study each sermon, you will soon be convinced that the central theme of early church preaching was the resurrection. They did not try to prove the resurrection; they used the fact of it to prove their claims for Christ. They felt no need of proving the resurrection. They had seen it and they reported what they saw, apparently satisfying their audiences.

The testimony of reliable eyewitnesses is considered sufficient by historians and by juries to establish truth. And there is nothing in the evidence to impugn the reliability of these eyewitnesses. They were rough, practical men, inclined to skepticism, easily cowed. The Jewish leaders who condemned their Master never did fathom their sudden boldness and conviction — there was no natural explanation for it, and they refused the obvious one.

The scientific method is not able to attest the fact of the resurrection because the resurrection is a one-time phenomenon which cannot be reproduced by laboratory experimentation. The processes of historical inquiry, however, force the openminded investigator to accept it as the best attested fact in all of ancient history.

In his biography, C. S. Lewis relates the story concerning an atheist who liked to compare the resurrection of Christ with all the ancient myths from pagan religions which centered around dying and rising gods. These were usually agricultural deities whose work of providing fruitfulness was symbolized by their dying after the harvest each year and rising in time for the new planting season. When this atheist studied the historical evidence in connection with the resurrection, he was forced to ask in awe: "What if it really did happen once?"

Another highly educated man, this one a lawyer, named Frank Morison, was tired of pretending in church to recite the phrase from the Apostles Creed, "On the third day He rose again from the dead." He decided, therefore, to put the claims for the resurrection to an exhaustive legal test.

The result of his inquiry is a little book entitled *Who Moved The Stone?*[71] Dr. Morison does not appear, at least from the evidence in this book, to accept the New Testament record as a supernaturally inspired writing. He uses it purely as he would any other established and trustworthy historical source material. From this viewpoint alone, he has written a fascinating document in which he establishes a conclusion that by all the rules of legal evidence the resurrection must be accepted as an undeniable historical fact.

Ever since the enemies of Christ first put forth their official version of the incident — that His disciples stole His body (Matthew 28:15) — attempts have been made to find acceptable alternatives to the fact that He actually did rise from the dead. One of the newest is written by a New Testament scholar reared in an orthodox Jewish home. Entitled *The Passover Plot*, it is an elaborate variation of the old swoon theory. This farfetched explanation suggests that Jesus deliberately set the stage for His dramatic death and resurrection by enlisting the aid of Joseph of Arimathea and other supporters. His idea was to goad the authorities into crucifying Him just before the Passover so that He would have to be taken from the cross before being there long enough to die. An accomplice would give Him a drug known to produce a trancelike state resembling death. He would allow Himself to be buried and later rescued. Schonfield concludes that His disciples succeeded in rescuing Him from the tomb but that He died a short time later from the effects of the unanticipated side wound and was then secretly buried.[72]

When we consider besides the wounds, the loss of blood, the weakened condition of one who had been through what Jesus had, it obviously would have taken nearly as much of a miracle to move the heavy stone (sealed with the official Roman seal and guarded by men whose lives depended on keeping it safe), to be rid of the constricting grave clothes, to overcome the overpowering scent of spices. Certainly the craven disciples who would not believe the truth even when they saw it, were no assistance in such a scheme. And if they had been, they would not have staked their lives on such a deception.

Some said the apostles were seeing things, or having hallucinations. The accusation is still made by those who want to deny the fact. But these were not men given to hallucinations. Oddly enough, one of their own number accused them, in effect, of that very thing. Thomas said seeing was not enough; he had to be able to touch before he would be convinced. Yet this one who wouldn't be taken in was soon one of those who believed (John 20:24-28).

This hallucination theory is the weakest of all those proposed as an alternate explanation of what really happened, because it does not take into account the undeniable fact of the empty tomb. The enemies of Christ could have quickly and easily disposed of it by showing that the grave still contained a body. Any acceptable alternative theory must account for both the apostles' testimony and the empty tomb.

The official explanation was that the disciples stole the body. That story was still being used when Matthew wrote, perhaps thirty years after the event (28:11). Since men will not devote their lives to a deliberate deception and certainly not die for it — they had nothing to gain by sticking to it — its weakness has been apparent to critics ever since. Rather than admit the truth, the search for a better explanation has gone on.

Another suggestion is that enemies stole the body of Jesus in order to keep it from becoming a shrine. It is weak on the face of it when one considers the strenuous efforts these enemies later made to stamp out the faith. They could have effectively conquered merely by producing the body or evidence of its disposal. This would have destroyed the foundation on which the Christian faith was built.

Some have suggested that in their distraught condition, the disciples went to the wrong tomb, and not finding what they expected, yielded to an excitement born of false hope. This, too, would soon have been clarified, either by the disciples when their emotions cooled, or by the authorities who would have taken pains to squelch the rumor.

Why the apostles later suffer persecution and martyrdom rather than admit fraud and foreswear their faith in the resurrected Christ, Schonfield and other explanation-seekers do not say. Neither is it clear what they think they hoped to gain from maintaining the fraud. This theory — like the predecessors on which it builds, proves only one thing — that every attempt to explain the resurrection in terms more palatable to the natural mind is so weak and unsatisfactory that each generation of unbelievers feels impelled to suggest a better one.

Those who feel a necessity to remove the resurrection from its place as the pivot of history, have come to grips with two embarrassing and irrefutable facts: 1) that the tomb was empty; 2) that a large number of people with nothing but persecution to gain staked everything on the conviction that they had seen Him alive. One or the other of these facts might be explained away: together they form an undeniable proof sufficient for the intellect of the openminded. Those who seek other explanations are not openminded. Either they are seeking how to do away with the necessity of facing Christ and making a decision for Him, or they start with the premise that since the resurrection is contrary to human experience and the science of biology, there must be some natural explanations for the facts. They only need to find what it is.

The appearances of Christ were not limited to a few occasions immediately following the crucifixion when the disciples were distraught and the women perhaps hysterical. The few examples given by the Gospel writers mention only the initial appearances, and even then He talked and ate and was handled; He was no temporary ghost produced by overwrought imaginations. But Acts 1 goes further. Our Lord had a task for His followers which implied no less than life and death commitment and a willingness to stake all on the conviction that they had ultimate truth to spread throughout the world.

Thus, for forty days He associated Himself with them, convincing them by "many infallible proofs" that He was indeed alive and not something they imagined in the hectic hours when they had fully succumbed to grief. This truth was the basis of all their sermons as it was later of Paul's. Even the enemies of the Christians knew that the resurrection was the foundation doctrine that made them so stubborn in clinging to their faith.

There has been found near the site of ancient Nazareth an old Roman inscription which proclaimed that on orders from Caesar anyone who desecrated a grave or removed a body was to suffer capital punishment. The best historical evidence dates this inscription to Caesar Claudius (about A.D. 40).[73] It is known that Claudius was upset by Jewish disturbances in Rome which on investigation proved to be caused by disagreement over one "Chrestus." For a time even, he banished the Jews from the city (Acts 18:2). And why would this inscription have been set up — the only place where such a one is known — in the far away and unimportant provincial town of Nazareth? The best guess is that Claudius, having investigated the disturbances and ascertaining that the sect of Nazarenes claimed their leader had risen from the dead and that their opponents claimed the body had been stolen, took action to forestall any more such incidents. Since Nazareth may have seemed to Claudius to be the birthplace of the movement, it was logical place to set up such a decree.

Even the enemies of Christianity knew (and still know) that to destroy it they must destroy belief in the resurrection, for this was the foundation and cornerstone of the faith of the church. The primary qualification of an apostle was that he was an eyewitness to the resurrection (Acts 1:22). The Christians believed in Christ because they believed He had risen. As C.S. Lewis says: "To preach Christianity meant primarily to preach the Resurrection . . . . The first fact in the history of Christendom is a number of people who say they have seen the Resurrection. If they had died without making anyone else believe this gospel, no Gospels would ever have been written."[74]

One thing explains the empty tomb, the careers of the apostles, and the birth of the church, and that thing is that Christ "rose from the dead according to the Scriptures."

"IF CHRIST BE NOT RISEN"

It is quite possible to know that Attila sacked Rome, that King John signed the Magna Charta at Runnymede, and that Washington crossed the Delaware, without having the tenor of one's life changed. One's attitudes and outlook may be untouched by these historic facts. But once the truth of the resurrection is accepted, one must come to grips with it. The Christian faith and the

Christian church are built on the resurrection as it is prophesied in Scripture, fulfilled in Christ, and proclaimed by the apostles. Once we admit these facts, we are admitting that God has uniquely set His seal of approval on Christ and on all He taught and did. When we admit all this, we are faced with a decision that we cannot sidestep. Either we submit to the One who is Lord of life and death and become a new creation (II Corinthians 5:17), or we defy Him, saying, "We will not have this man to reign over us" (Luke 19:14), choosing deterioration of character, cynicism, and hopelessness.

Paul did not spend much time trying to prove the resurrection. The Scriptures had foretold it, and the eyewitnesses — including himself — had seen Christ alive. The thing to discuss was not the fact of the resurrection but the implications of it. Two things, Paul said, hinge on it. If Christ has not risen, your sins have not been forgiven and you have no hope (I Corinthians 15:17). In other words, you are staking your life on a vain faith Paul himself had become a Christian, not because of the beautiful character or lofty teachings of Christ, but solely because the resurrected Christ revealed Himself to Paul.

If the resurrection is less than a fact, the faith of the saints has been an idle dream. "If Christ be not raised . . . ye are yet in your sins," Paul said in I Corinthians 15:17.

Jesus said His blood was shed for the remission of sins, but who would believe it had He remained in the tomb? He died under a curse, for the law said, "Cursed is everyone that hangeth on a tree" (Deuteronomy 21:23; Galatians 3:13). We could never be sure He was taking our curse had God not vindicated Him by raising Him up. Death came with sin and the main proof that He was not a sinner, as other men, is that death could not conquer Him. For though it is His death that makes our atonement, it is His resurrection that justifies our faith that this is so.

Without the resurrection, the cross is robbed of its

meaning. It becomes a tragic error, a miscarriage of justice, a mere martydom. Jesus becomes only a man with lofty ideals and delusions of grandeur. But by the resurrection God with one stroke declared it all true. Jesus was all He claimed to be; the wages of sin had been paid forever, and believing mankind was free from the penalty of sin. Christ was conqueror over death and the grave. The Christian can face death knowing that he will be immediately in the presence of the resurrected victorious Christ for all eternity.

Through the resurrection there is certainty of the day when our bodies will be raised and made like unto His glorious body. There is the promise of an existence where wrongs will be righted and sin will be forever banished. There is certainty of reunion with those loved ones who have died in Christ. "We sorrow not as those who have no hope," Paul wrote in I Thessalonians 4:13-18. Death is not final. The grave is not the end because Christ's resurrection was a literal, bodily resurrection.

If Christ be not raised, those who preach Him have increased their burden of sin by becoming false witnesses. The apostles staked everything on the truth of their testimony that they had seen Christ alive. Paul "suffered the loss of all things" (Philippians 3:8) for his conviction that he had seen the risen Christ. Thousands of Christians throughout the Roman Empire suffered torture and death rather than give up their assurance of forgiveness and eternal life. Polycarp, pupil of the Apostle John, was burned at the stake in Ephesus when he was an old man. Given a last minute opportunity to recant, he said: "Eighty and six years have I served Him and He has done me naught but good. Shall I deny Him now?" Someone has said that a roll call of twentieth-century martyrs would be even longer than those of the early church. Even now, after nearly two thousand years, there are millions who know He is alive and has forgiven their sins. On this knowledge they stake everything.

If there were no resurrection, there could be no Christians. Romans 10:9 is unequivocal concerning this. It stands in spite of the fact that Jefferson said his emasculated gospel proved he was a *real* Christian. It stands even though Rudolf Bultmann, who says the resurrection is not a historical event, is considered a leading Christian theologian. It stands, regardless of Albert Schweitzer's statement, that the resurrection is legendary and unnecessary to the truths which Jesus taught.

If Christ be not risen we do not know whether there is a resurrection or a future life. If this life is all, then obviously the best thing to do is "eat and drink" and be merry (I Corinthians 15:32) and enjoy it as much as possible. Paul and others who had given up all that seems good and worthwhile in this life were the most miserable of all men if they were building on a vain hope. In verses 30-32, he mentions a few of the ills he had already endured (and when this was written another ten years of labor and suffering were still ahead of him). Yet Paul is the last person one would ever call miserable. Notice at the end of the chapter how he rises to a crescendo of joy (verses 55-58) as he completes his contemplation of the resurrection and all it has meant and will yet mean to him.

Not only for our personal outlook does the resurrection bring assuring hope, but for us who believe, hope soars from the ashes of grief. To the bereaved, it is written in I Thessalonians 4:13 that we "sorrow not, even as others which have no hope." Painful as it is, separation is not final for those who know of a resurrection and future eternal reunion.

A well-to-do but unhappy woman in India heard for the first time about Christ. As she listened to His wonderful deeds and love and compassion, she said, "Oh, how I could love Him; I have longed for such a God." But as she was told of the crucifixion, her face fell. "Then He is dead," she said, "there is no hope to be had in a dead man." The missionary hastened to finish the story, telling of the resurrection and of Christ's own words: "I am He that liveth, and was dead; and, behold, I am alive for evermore" (Revelation 1:18). So one more soul found hope and joy in the knowledge of a God and Saviour who is really alive.

It has long been customary among eastern Christians to greet one another on Easter morning by saying, "Christ is Risen!" and to receive the joyous response, "He is risen indeed!" In spite of the vocal minority of those who proclaim that God is dead, we stand firm and respond with assurance, "He lives! He is alive forevermore!"

12

THE MIRACLE OF PAUL
Evidence from Psychology

It was the Age of Reason. So men styled the mid-eighteenth century in which they lived. Two Englishmen, one a lawyer and the other a member of the Parliament, sat discussing Christianity and their own reasons for unbelief. Surely, by reason alone they could demonstrate the impossibility of the ancient faith and show the Bible to be a fraud. They agreed that each would choose a miracle and demonstrate its incredibility. Gilbert West would show that the resurrection of Christ could not have happened, and George Lyttelton would demonstrate the conversion of Paul to be a fraud. They parted with great confidence and enthusiasm, agreeing that at their next meeting each would present his case to the other. To their amazement, when they came together, they each discovered that the other had been converted by his studies and had written in defense rather than in criticism of his subject.

Samuel Johnson, in his critique of Lyttelton's writings,[75] calls it "a treatise to which infidelity has never been able to fabricate a specious answer." He also relates how Lyttelton's father, surprised and pleased by his son's paper, wrote him, "I have read your religious treatise with infinite pleasure and satisfaction . . . . I shall never cease glorifying God for having endowed you with such wonderful talents and giving me so good a son." George, who subsequently was elevated to the peerage as a baron and is remembered as Lord Lyttelton, entitled his paper, "Observations on the Conversion and Apostleship of St. Paul," with the subtitle, "A Letter to Gilbert West, Esq."[76]

A discussion in *Life* magazine of the contribution of the Apostle Paul[77] opens this way: "In the history of our culture few individuals have been as influential as Paul, the First Century Jew who turned from being the most virulent persecutor of Christianity to become its most powerful advocate, its most effective interpreter and the leader of its triumphant march across the ancient world." It is, in fact, impossible to conceive of our civilization developing as it has if Paul were removed from it. Open any history book on world cultures or western civilization or ancient history, and you will find him given prominent coverage. He was one of the few great creative personalities on whom history hinges and without whom it would surely have developed far differently.

PAUL THE JEW

The Christian church boasts many remarkable and pivotal conversions that have changed the course of history. One thinks immediately of the Emperor Constantine. Such also was the conversion of King Clovis of the Franks, resulting in Frankish championship of the rising Papacy. Similarly, the conversion of Ethelbert, king of Kent, through Augustine, led to the conversion of the Anglo-Saxons. In more recent times, the acceptance of the Christian faith by Queen Kapiolani of Hawaii, followed by her dramatic descent into a volcano's mouth to challenge the goddess believed to inhabit it, abated the deep-seated fear of her subjects and turned them to Christ in great numbers. It is hoped that the conversion of the Auca killers and of tribal chieftains such as Tariri and Elka will be likewise pivotal for the people of the Amazon jungles.

Certainly the conversion of Saul of Tarsus ranks next to the work of Christ as the most important event in Christendom. It is a convincing evidence to the fact of the resurrection and the truth of the gospel. Apart from it we have no adequate explanation for the existence of the church in its human organized form. We who are Gentiles should continually praise God for giving us so great an apostle to undertake the third phase of the great commission, "and unto the uttermost part of the earth" (Acts 1:8), to where it would ultimately reach us.

What made Paul a pivotal individual? Only his experience on the road to Damascus explains his life, the existence of the church as we know it, and his impact on subsequent history. His conversion is a climax which gives meaning and direction to all his previous life and understanding for all that follows.

Probably no one could be better fitted for the work to which he was called than the Apostle Paul. It has been said that he was a citizen of three worlds — the Jewish, the Greek, and the Roman. Though born into a wealthy and prominent Jewish family that had attained the priceless boon of Roman citizenship, Paul grew up in a Gentile city and was thoroughly at home with Greek language and culture. As the son of a Pharisee (Acts 23:6), however, he was educated in the strictest manner of orthodox Judaism and had a knowledge of the Old Testament that was both deep and extensive. His teacher was the illustrious Rabbi Gamaliel (Acts 22:3) with whom his personality, however, was in sharp contrast. Gamaliel is pictured as temporizing with a "wait and see" policy concerning the followers of Jesus (Acts 5:34-39) at the same time that his young student, Paul the activist, is out with all the vigor of a true believer in Judaism doing everything he can to stamp out the new faith (Acts

8:1-3; 9:1,2; Galatians 1:13,14; Philippians 3:6). This would be quite in character for a young man referred to in the *Talmud* as "that pupil" who is said to have caused the Elder Gamaliel considerable trouble, manifesting "impudence in matters of Learning." Joseph Klausner, who comments on the entry, goes on to say, "Jesus is called in ancient Hebrew literature 'that man' and only Paul could have been intended by the words 'that pupil' — the pupil of Rabban Gamaliel who 'went wrong' and thus could not be mentioned by name."[78]

Undoubtedly he knew the Scriptures in both Hebrew and Greek. He astounded the Roman tribune with his cultured Greek and stilled the mob by his use of Aramaic when he was rescued in the temple (Acts 21:37-40). He was a brilliant controversialist, ambitious, opinionated, zealous and devout. As an orator of quality, he could hold his own in such diverse places as the Temple in Jerusalem and the Areopagus in Athens. On several occasions, Luke refers to the use Paul made of his hands while speaking (Acts 13:16; 21:40). He was unquestionably honest in his efforts to serve God.

Though Paul was not a Greek by nationality, he was a citizen of Tarsus, a Greek metropolis which controlled the Cilician Gates, the famous passage through the Taurus Mountains. These mountains form a protective wall across eastern Asia Minor, effectively separating it from the rest of Asia. Whoever controls the Gates controls Asia Minor. Through the centuries the armies of the Hittites, Assyrians, Persians, Greeks (led by Alexander the Great), and later the Romans, Byzantines, Crusaders, and Turks have moved to and fro through it. Saul's home town of Tarsus commanded the eastern approaches to this vital pass and grew wealthy on the trade that flowed through it. Naturally, it was a mixture of Greek and Oriental elements where one could learn from both worlds. Here Paul was taught Greek, and probably became familiar with the Septuagint version of the Old Testament which he was to quote frequently in his epistles. Here also was the University of Tarsus to which Apollonodorus, teacher and advisor to the Emperor Augustus, had retired.

Above all, Paul possessed Roman citizenship, a privilege not to be taken lightly in the ancient world. In the first century A.D. few outside Italy enjoyed this prize. Perhaps some ancestor had done some great service for a passing Roman Commander. All Paul tells us is that he was Roman born. It gave him unusual prestige and not infrequently got him out of a jam. Other men paid tremendous sums of money to become Roman citizens. Acts 22:25-30 gives us a little insight to this in the comment of the chief captain who tells how he obtained his Roman citizenship.

This passport gave him access and protection that no other apostle had. Whenever the Jews of a community brought charges against him, he had only to produce it to get a hearing before the highest Roman authority. Archaeology has over and over shown us that the author of Acts invariably used the correct titles in each of these cases. His trial at Corinth can be exactly dated to A.D. 51, since Gallio, brother of Seneca the famous philosopher and advisor to Nero, had only one year there as governor and erected a monument dating it, which has been found at Delphi.[79]

Paul's conversion was the dominant event of his life. Acts gives us three accounts of it, first as history (Acts 9), and twice as he tells it in personal testimonies (Acts 22 and 26). No doubt he told it frequently; perhaps even before Nero Caesar.

Although critics find contradictions in these accounts, the small variations are entirely differences of emphasis such as naturally appear when telling the same story to different audiences. The first is the third person account of a historian, simply presenting an orderly story of the most important conversion in the early church and preparing the reader for Paul's later prominent role. In the second (Acts 22), Paul faces a fanatical Jewish mob that has branded him a traitor and blasphemer. He recounts his life and claims his conversion is a revelation in which God has ordered him to do what he has done. It is spoken in the familiar format of the Old Testament prophets' account of their calls. The conclusion of the argument is lost in the shouts of the mob.

The third account resembles the second more than the first. Its differences may be explained by the fact that the situation is less heated, Paul begging before a supposedly impartial court rather than a mob and defending himself against the charge of being a disturber of the peace. This time he is permitted to finish the argument, which is presented in a manner suitable to the dignity of the hearers. He indicates that he cannot disobey this heavenly vision and, therefore, he has presented the gospel of Christ to the Gentiles. If Paul's accounts had been contradictory, Luke as a historian would have noticed and checked his points for accuracy.

The fact that Lord Lyttelton considered Paul's conversion as next to the resurrection a basic linchpin in the edifice of Christian doctrine, and that even now critics who wish to destroy the validity of the faith concentrate their attacks on it, is an important evidence to its centrality in the Christian revelation The radical nature of Christian conversion is as much a miracle as anything in Scripture. It simply cannot be credited by those who have not experienced it and so they seek psychological explanations for the undeniable change which took place — he fell off his horse, or had a nightmare, or a sunstroke. That none of these common occurrences produce such permanent results in others, they do not explain.

A popular suggestion is that a bolt of lightning frightened him. After all, didn't lightning so frighten Martin Luther that he abandoned law to enter a monastery? They fail to see that Luther's case was not a conversion, or even a real change of direction, but merely a stepped-up effort on his part to please God by his own efforts. Conversion came later to Luther after his superior assigned him to study Scripture and take over some university Bible courses. (Another evidence of the inherent power in God's Word!)

A real favorite is the suggestion that Paul had an epileptic seizure as he approached Damascus. Did he not have an unnamed "thorn in the flesh" (II Corinthians 12:7)? With effort, as good a case can be made for epilepsy as for any of several other maladies (eye disease, malaria, and a grotesque appearance all have their supporters). But of the hundreds of attacks of a typical epileptic in a lifetime, no one has explained why this one should result in so phenomenal a change of direction. Nor is there any record that he was so subject. Paul does describe a vision in the Temple (Acts 22:17,18), but no one accuses Peter of epilepsy because of his vision (Acts 10:11). Of the experience outside Lystra, one can only say that stoning is of itself an unusual experience.

No fall, or sunstroke, or epileptic seizure, or lightning bolt would produce more than a brief hallucination. Paul did not travel alone; he had servants with him, perhaps a companion, and certainly one or two officers prepared to guard any prisoners sent back to Jerusalem. These would have been aware of any such conjectured incident and capable of telling him he had suffered some temporary derangement by reason of a concussion or epileptic attack. But Paul, to the end of his days, was firm in his conviction that he had been in full control of his wits and literally had seen the risen Christ, who personally commissioned him. In listing the resurrection appearances in I Corinthians 15:5-8, he adds, "And last of all he was seen of me also." No opposition or suffering was sufficient to cause him to look back or doubt his destiny.

Saul was well versed in the Law. He knew the test of a true prophet given in Deuteronomy 18:20-22. It is noteworthy, therefore, to notice how his vision was confirmed to him by prophetic characteristics. Like Zacharias, who became dumb, Paul was struck blind until it was fulfilled. He had a second vision informing him of the name of the one who would heal him (Acts 9:12). Also, Ananias had to be persuaded to go to heal Paul because he had every earthly reason to believe he was going to his own destruction.

Even less reasonable is the argument that Paul deliberately staged his conversion because he saw some advantage in joining the Christians. He had security and every advantage for which men strive; he was already recognized as a leader. He was prominent in leading Pharisaic circles and had the confidence of the authorities. His family was respected and his connections impeccable. With his genius in debate, so admired by the Pharisees, he probably would have gone down in the Talmud as one of the great Rabbans and have been extensively quoted. He had everything to lose and nothing to gain by his conversion and, in fact, says that as a result of it he suffered the loss of all things (Philippians 3:7,8). No doubt, this includes disinheritance by his family as well as rejection by the Jewish leaders who had considered him to hold such great promise.

Furthermore, had he only become intellectually convinced that the Christian position was correct, he would have remained the same Saul serving a different cause. But the intolerant, persecuting Pharisee, Saul, enforcing conformity by coercion, became Paul the man of large sympathy and understanding, desiring to persuade men to a deep faith.

Conversion is, as the word implies, a turning around from one destination to its exact opposite, involving a radical change in attitude, ambition, and personality. Paul's conversion exemplified all this to the highest degree. Such change is not the result of hallucination, illness, or fright. He had literally become what he later called all Christians, "a new creature" (II Corinthians 5:17).

Those who seek psychological suggestions for Paul's conversion forget that he changed more than his opinion of Christianity or even his understanding of who Christ is. Never again would he seek merely to establish his personal belief by forcing outward conformity through coercion and fear. His whole heart and entire inner nature were changed, and this same change was what he sought in others. To accomplish this he would persuade men, not persecute them. He had hated Christians (was "exceedingly mad" against them, Acts 26:11) but now toward those who opposed him he expressed only love and the desire to have them share in the priceless forgiveness he had found. Obedience to the living Christ became his obsession.

Many and varied modern conversions demonstrate a complete about-face on the part of individuals. Dr. Reuben Archer Torrey, the well-known evangelist and Bible teacher during the earlier part of the twentieth century, is a case in point. When he was a young man, he was deep in sin, though his mother was a devout Christian. She had prayed many years for him and had talked often to him about the Saviour. One day in deep agitation Dr. Torrey told his mother he was tired of hearing her continual pleadings to accept the Lord, and he was going to leave home so that he would bother her no longer. His mother followed him to the gate, pleading and weeping, urging him to turn to the Lord, but he would not listen. Her parting words to him were, "Son, when you come to the darkest hour of all, when everything seems lost and gone, if you will earnestly call on your mother's God and seek Him, you will get help."

Having left the influence of home and mother R.A. Torrey went farther and farther from God and deeper and deeper into sin. One night in a hotel room he was unable to sleep. As he lay thinking, he became convinced that life was not worth living, sin did not satisfy and there was no relief in sight. Still unable to get to sleep, he made the decision to use the gun on his dresser to end his life. On his way to pick up the gun those parting words of his mother flashed into his troubled mind.

The disturbed young man dropped to his knees alongside his bed and cried out, "Oh, God of my mother, if there be such a Being, I want help. I want light. If you will give it to me, I will follow You!"

There was no blinding flash of light, no audible voice, but in answer to his cry the Lord quieted his soul and filled his heart with peace and light. In those moments by that hotel bedside R.A. Torrey made a business transaction with God that changed the entire course and purpose of his life. He accepted Jesus Christ, the resurrected Saviour, as his Lord and then hurried home to tell his mother. Upon his appearance she said, "Oh, my boy, I knew you were coming back! You have found the Lord! God has told me so!"

Those who have not experienced conversion can neither understand nor explain the radical change it produces. They try to find a pigeonhole for it within the framework of their experience. Paul stands astride history, and he must be accounted for. The New Testament and the church exist, and they must be accounted for. One outstanding evidence for the truth of the resurrection and the entire Christian revelation is the fact that Paul came face to face with the living Christ and was not only changed but changed the face of civilization by his active and fruitful ministry.

PAUL THE CHRISTIAN

Of those who seek excuses to avoid conversion to Christ, some have said, "If I had an experience like Paul's, I might become a Christian." Such arrogance! They forget Paul was unique among all the recorded conversions in the New Testatment. They also forget he was an honest man diligently serving God with a clear conscience according to his best understanding. When God showed him he was wrong, he abandoned his course, heedless of personal cost, and followed truth. One who willfully rejects Christ has no right to compare himself to the great apostle.

Paul, like the other apostles, is in the prophetic succession. Abraham, with whom God shared His plans; Moses, whom He knew face to face; Samuel, who heard His voice as a child; Elijah, who demonstrated His power; Isaiah, who saw His glory; Jeremiah, chosen before his conception; Daniel, who saw the Ancient of Days; and later John on Patmos. These were all chosen instruments of infallible revelation, ordained to bring God's Word to man. Paul, to whom we owe a large portion of the New Testament, is of their company and like them was given an abundance of revelations (II Corinthians 12:7).

Why was Paul granted so unusual a conversion? He himself had no doubt but that he was a chosen vessel, predestined to a special purpose. He was in the exclusive company of the prophets and apostles — those granted infallible revelation in order that God's message might be made known to men. All his background — education, citizenship, knowledge of language, understanding of Jewish and Greek culture, even witnessing Stephen's death — had been planned by an omnipotent God towards this one end, that he might be builder of Christ's church among the Gentiles.

Before Paul's birth God's purposes were formed in him — in the choice of his family, his home town, his citizenship. Without his Jewish heritage and knowledge of the Jewish Scriptures he could not have fully understood the work and sacrifice of Jesus the Messiah, nor grasped the centrality of the crucifixion for all mankind. Without his understanding of Greek language and culture he could not have presented Christ so as to make Him meaningful to those who lacked a Hebrew background. Without his

Roman citizenship he could not have moved so freely throughout the Empire and planted churches in all its provinces.

Obedience was both the immediate and lasting evidence and result of Paul's conversion. From the moment he met the Lord, he sought His will. "Lord, what wilt thou have me to do?" he asked. The Lord answered his question then and continued to answer it with each step Paul took. And Paul continued to listen and obey.

As is always the case with a true revelation, it was built on previous revelation. God does not contradict Himself. Notice the parallel between Christ's command in Acts 1:8, and Paul's description of his obedience in Acts 27:19,20.

The course of Paul's life was shaped before he was called, and when called, he was prepared to obey. His conversion was his unalterable defense. Because of it he was Christ's bondslave, in debt and under orders. "I was not disobedient to the heavenly vision" (Acts 26:19), he told Agrippa. His singlemindedness cannot be explained except in the light of his conversion experience. But when that is understood, all that follows is inevitable.

Paul was a chosen vessel to establish the church in the uttermost part of the world. He planted the faith in western Asia and Europe; and wherever the restless Europeans have gone in their search for gold or land or adventure, they have taken the cross and the culture that was built on it. It would be easier today to explain the New World without Columbus or the United States without Washington than to explain the church in its corporate, visible form without Paul. Paul's life and accomplishments evidence the supernatural reality of his conversion. And his conversion is, next to the resurrection, most truly our greatest and most miraculous Christian evidence.

13

LIVING EVIDENCE
Evidence from Changed Lives

Perhaps you come to this last chapter with a feeling that man's researches have so thoroughly vindicated the Bible that no one can fail to believe it is truly God's infallible revelation to man and to accept its message. Or perhaps you know someone who is familiar with all these evidences and more but who still refuses to acknowledge the claims of Christ. Such an attitude is hard to understand, especially when you know your faith stands firm even without such proof. But remember there are many who want to believe the Word of God, especially young people who may be thrown into confusion by agnostic teachers. These individuals need and appreciate Christian evidences. Why do so many others refuse to take the step of faith even when their questions and doubts have been fully answered? The Lord answers this question in II Corinthians 4:4,5. Satan, the god of this age, has blinded their eyes.

A group of students at a large university had gathered to discuss the question, "Does a Supreme Being govern life?" They agreed that every religion and people in the world recognize a Supreme Being. Then one countered, "But Christians today live as if God didn't." Evidently he had never seen a Christian who let the Supreme Being govern his life.

A grandmother, freed from the responsibility of rearing children, took a job to fill the long hours. One day, during a discussion she offered a book to a co-worker, feeling it would explain the Christian message better than she could. The friend took it and later said, "There are others in this office who call themselves Christians and I wouldn't even take a book from them, let alone read it. But I notice you live what you believe and I'd like to learn more about it from you."

NO FEAR OF GOD

Belief in God and a transforming faith are not necessarily synonymous. Lord Moran accompanied Winston Churchill to Moscow as his personal physician when Churchill had the unpleasant task of breaking the bad news to Stalin that there would be no invasion of Europe in 1942. The Russian was visibly unhappy at receiving no relief from German pressure. Then Churchill described the plans for stepped-up bombing of Germany, and finally revealed to him the plans for the invasion of North Africa. When he finished, Stalin, in a much better mood, said, "May God prosper this undertaking." When Churchill related this conversation to Lord Moran, the doctor asked, "Did he really say that?"

"Oh," replied the Prime Minister, "he brings in the deity quite a lot."[80]

Similarly surprising, former Russian Premier Nikita Kruschev memorized large quantities of Scripture as a youth and enjoyed quoting it, but it apparently was nothing more than a mental exercise.

Lip service to a Supreme Being, even from the chief of an officially atheist government, is not enough to make a man a Christian. James said, "The devils believe and tremble" (James 2:19). Stalin's awareness of God was obviously quite shallow.

If belief in God is not sufficient to save a man, what is necessary? We saw in the case of Paul that conversion to Christ so changed him that others knew he had been in contact with a living Person.

Even many who profess to believe in God fail to acknowledge with reverence and gratitude the Creator and Sustainer of all things. For this they are without excuse because His identity has been made plain on all of His creation. As David in the Psalms has said, "The heavens declare the glory of God; and the firmament showeth his handywork" (Psalm 19:1). Thus, as Romans 3 tells us, "There is none righteous . . . there is none that doeth good." Why? Because mankind does not want "to retain God in its knowlege" (Romans 1:28) and so closes his eyes deliberately to the evidence. Instead, he seeks natural explanations, missing links, or natural causes.

God went further and sought to make Himself plain to man by revealing Himself in Christ and in the Scripture. And because the natural man still prefers to live without God, he spurns even this revelation. Thus it is that Christian evidences are not infallibly convincing. Christian apologists cannot convince men against their wills. The criticisms we have studied in this course were raised by those who did not want to submit their wills to God and so sought to nullify the force of His revelation by raising objections to it.

Sound scholarship has answered critical objections. Archaeological knowledge has revealed to us the backgrounds of Genesis so that they can no longer be called legendary and has demonstrated the wisdom of God's dealing with the Canaanites. It has vindicated the Mosaic authorship of the Pentateuch and has brought to light long-forgotten kingdoms, kings, conquerors. Geographical studies have shown that the lands of the Bible are accurately described, and no research of modern science has been able to prove the Scripture in a scientific error. The reality of the supernatural has been evidenced by miracles and prophecies. The life of Christ, His resurrection, the work and writing of Paul and the other apostles have all been demonstrated to be historical realities. Yet, despite all this, unbelief still persists and some go far as to proclaim that God is dead.

Is not such a proclamation merely an effort to escape the fact "that they are all under sin" (Romans 3:9)? Is it not an effort to justify situation ethics and make right whatever sin they wish to enjoy? As Paul said, "There is no fear of God before their eyes" (Romans 3:18). It is only by accepting God's revealed Word that we are aware that "all have sinned, and come short of the glory of God" (Romans 3:23).

Man does not like to retain God in his knowledge. This is what the Bible says, and it is one answer as to why man needs more and more evidences. He has always been surrounded by evidences. He has always been surrounded by evidences of the Creator, and he has always willfully shut his eyes to them. Was this not true of Adam and Eve? Get knowledge, Satan told them, and you will be like God (Genesis 3:5). Did not Pharaoh harden his heart and refuse to believe the evidences of God's power when he saw it working through Moses?

Remember the story of King Ahaz? He was afraid because the kings of Samaria and Damascus had plotted to overthrow him and set up a puppet king, and so he sought an alliance with the powerful Assyrians to help him defend himself against them. Isaiah warned him it was a mistake. The strength of Ahaz and of Judah was not in Assyria but in God. In a few short years the two kingdoms that he so feared would disapper. Their evil schemes against Ahaz would come to naught. He was safe because he embodied the line of David to whom had been promised the throne forever. To clinch his message, Isaiah said God would give Ahaz as a sign anything he might ask. Ahaz at that moment virtually had a blank check on the power of God. But the king had made up his mind.

He would sign the treaty with Assyria and all would be well. He did not want to give up his own will, and so he did not want evidence that God's power and promise were his sufficient protection. "No thank you," he said in effect to Isaiah. "I will not test God by asking a sign" (Isaiah 7:12). In short, no amount of evidence from God would change his mind.

The Jews of Jesus' day did not want to believe. Throughout His entire ministry He had given evidences to the fact that He was the promised Messiah. The fair-minded Nicodemus, when interviewing Him, recognized that "no man can do these miracles that thou doest, except God be with him" (John 3:2). Yet the unbelieving Jews had the arrogance to say to Him on one occasion, "Show us a sign and we will believe you" (John 6:30). This was immediately after seeing Him feed the five thousand men. The chief priests and Pharisees sent officers to check further. Their report was "Never man spake like this man" (John 7:46). So they accused them of being deceived and supported their rejection by saying that none of the rulers believed on Him. When Nicodemus spoke up, giving that excuse the lie, they ridiculed even him and went their own way. Truly, as Jesus said on another occasion, "If they hear not Moses and the prophets, neither will they be persuaded, though one rose from the dead" (Luke 16:31).

The Bible says that man is without excuse (Romans 1:20). He refuses to accept evidence he does not want to accept. Yet he cannot avoid a life built on faith. When he refuses God's Word and bolsters his unbelief by resorting to the opinions of Bible critics, he is choosing to place his faith in their conclusions rather than in what God has said. Hebrews 11:6 says, "Without faith it is impossible to please him." We trust Him or we trust something else, and only when we choose to trust Him can we do His will.

But the man "convinced beyond his will is of the same

opinion still." Christian evidences will not help those who deliberately turn their backs on the knowledge of God, living as the Scripture passage says, "vain in their imaginations, . . . professing themselves wise," and "without excuse" (Romans 1:22,23).

Those who benefit from the evidence fall mainly into two groups. One is composed of Christians who cling to their Lord but are beset by questions when those who seem more learned give authoritative sounding judgments that the Bible is untrustworthy and full of errors. Such Christians take comfort in knowing that their faith is supported by reason, and often take courage to stand for their faith in the face of the carpers. Also in this group are young people of Christian rearing who are in the throes of seeking to make sure their faith is their own and not a family heritage passed on to them

In the other group is the honest doubter. He may have been taught only the criticisms of the Bible and mistaken them for fact. But when faced with another alternative, he approaches it with an open mind, putting aside any prior conclusion and honestly willing to submit to truth when it is shown him.

Lord Lyttelton was one such man. When writing his biography, Samuel Johnson said of him: "He had, in the pride of juvenile confidence, with the help of corrupt conversation, entertained doubts of the truth of Christianity; but he thought the time now come when it was no longer fit to doubt or believe by chance, and applied himself seriously to the great question. His studies, being honest, ended in conviction."[81] This of course, will be the end of every honest investigation into the truth.

Such a man also was Sir William Ramsay. Having been trained in the critical school's methods and beliefs, and taking the validity of them for granted, he set out for Turkey to demonstrate that Acts contained anachronisms which would prove it to be of second-century origin rather than first. As his researches progressed, his critical opinions had to be discarded and he came to be the champion of an early date for Acts. He was one of the foremost apologists of the early twentieth century.[82]

Such honesty is unfortunately too rare in scholarly circles. Once a stand has been taken, it seems necessary to defend it despite the weight of any new evidence. Whereas in the ancient world men "changed the glory of the incorruptible God into an image" (Romans 1:23) to worship, man now dispenses with temples and images made with hands, but worships man himself and his wisdom.

NEW CREATURES IN CHRIST

Christian evidences will not convince one who refuses to accept them, but there is one Christian evidence which no one can completely dismiss. Often it has been heeded when all other evidences are refused — the evidence of a genuinely changed life. Henry M. Stanley, who sought out David Livingstone in Africa and stayed with him some months, gave this testimony: "I went to Africa as prejudiced as the biggest atheists in London . . . . But little by little his [Livingstone's] sympathy for others became contagious; my sympathy was aroused; seeing his piety, his gentleness, his zeal, his earnestness, and how he went about his business, I was converted by him, although he had not tried to do it."[83]

A speaker once admonished a newly ordained group of ministers, "Young men, believe me, you will make more people Christians by being Christians yourself than you will by all the sermons you will ever preach."

Corinth was a bustling Greek commercial city with a great deal of wealth and a plentiful supply of temples to the various gods and goddesses. Drunkenness, immorality, and other forms of over-indulgence were accepted parts of the rituals honoring many of the gods, but in Corinth these excesses had gone so far that the name of the city became synonymous with evil throughout the Greek world. To call one a Corinthian was to suggest that one had sunk so far in immorality and self-indulgence as to be beyond the pale of even the licentious first-century Greek. It is no wonder that, with such a background as this, the church at Corinth caused Paul more heartaches than any other with their many stumblings and failures. "Such were some of you," Paul says after recounting the most typical sins of Corinth. "But now . . ." What a change that *now,* implied. The faith of the Corinthians had been the talk of the Roman world. In that licentious city, there was known to be a community of people whose lives were so radiantly beautiful against the ugliness of their surroundings that many inquired the cause, and on learning believed. Thus they multiplied the effect of Paul's preaching many times over.

It is frequently a godly person's living that attracts converts before preaching. One example is an African prince acting as interpreter for a missionary. Closing the sermon, he added on his own: "I cannot read so I do not know what this Book says. But I have watched the missionary for two years and he tells no lies so I know what he tells us about the message of this Book is true."

Those who refuse Christ because there are hypocrites in the church are really saying that they see no Christian evidence in the lives of those who profess to know Him.

Christian conversion is a radical change. Though such spectacular circumstances of conversion such as Paul's are unique, the results in Paul's attitude and personality are not unusual. Paul even explained the secret of this radical change to the Corinthian church. "If any man be in Christ, he is a new creature" (II Corinthians 5:17). Something completely new is formed whenever one cedes his will and life to Jesus Christ. So different is it that Jesus called it being born again — an absolutely fresh beginning. "Look," Paul exclaims, "everything is new!"

Where there is no significant change in the mental,

moral, and spiritual attitudes and actions, the professing Christian ought to reexamine his "experience" in the light of the Word of God to be sure he is genuinely born into the family of God.

Dr. Harry Ironside relates an incident from his early ministry when he visited a street meeting in San Francisco and was asked to speak. As he finished, a well-known agnostic handed up his business card on which he had written a challenge to debate "Agnosticism versus Christianity" at four o'clock the following Sunday.

Dr. Ironside read the invitation aloud and said, "I accept this challenge on condition you defend the worth of your belief by bringing to the platform with you one man who has been rescued by the power of your teaching to a useful life from the grip of some vice against which he was helpless, and one woman of deep immoral background who because of your philosophy is now a modest, pure, honorable member of society. For my part I will meet you with one hundred such witnesses to the power of Christ." Turning to the Salvation Army captain leading the meeting, he asked. "Can you help me gather them in time?"

"Indeed," she replied, "we can get at least forty from our chapter alone and provide a brass band escort."

"I'll be there at four," Ironside concluded, "leading my hundred witnesses to the tune of 'Onward, Christian Soldiers!'" The challenger smiled, waved his hand negatively, and eased his way out of the wildly applauding crowd.[84]

Dr. Ironside had produced the one argument which the most learned unbeliever cannot adequately answer. It is the responsibility of every Christian to be this kind of argument for the truth of his faith, and it is done merely by letting the life of Christ shine through. Sadhu Singh, an Indian evangelist, once compared Christians to the moon. "It has no light of its own, but only reflects the light of the sun to the earth. Sometimes, though, it gets between the sun and the world and eclipses the light."

The evidence of a transformed life has no rebuttal. Men have tried countless ways to change others for the better. Both punishment and rehabilitation fail. Social reform has disappointed its most ardent advocates. Often education only teaches cleverer ways to do wrong and get away with it. "Teach a pickpocket to write," Dr. Bob Jones, Sr. used to say, "and you will probably make a forger." Psychology has often left its patients more confused than it found them. Some drugs act on the personality, but they produce no new creations.

The unconverted expect those who make a Christian profession to be different, and they are repelled by a false testimony. "I might have become a Christian," a doctor told a personal worker, "if I had not met so many people who said they were." But the influence of one who really demonstrates a changed life is irresistible. A group of preachers were once comparing Bible translations when one said, "My favorite translation and the one which made me a minister is the way my mother translated the gospel by living it."

Are you a living evidence to the truth of the Christian gospel?

Perhaps you are not a Christian yet. You have adequate evidence that the Scriptures are the inspired Word of a holy God. In the light of this evidence you must make a decision — either to go on in your unbelief and sin or to accept them and act in accordance with them by placing your trust in the One of whom they speak.

The closer you look, the greater the book. If you have approached and sifted the evidence with an open mind you cannot help seeing that the facts prove beyond doubt that the Scriptures cannot be broken.

Notes

1. George Harkness, *Understanding the Christian Faith* (New York-Nashville: Abingdon-Cokesbury, 1947), p. 28.

2. Elmer Homrighausen, *Christianity in America: A Crisis* (New York: Abingdon Press, 1936).

3. Neo-orthodox is from the Greek *neos,* meaning new; *orthos,* meaning right or true; and *doxa,* meaning opinion. This is the position held by the theologically liberal groups.

4. Brinton, Christopher, and Wolff, *A History of Civilization* (Englewood Cliffs: Prentice-Hall, 1955), p. 39.

5. *National Geographic,* December, 1966.

6. This presentation of the four writers is greatly simplified. For those desiring additional information, *An Introduction to the Old Testament* by Edward J. Young, published by Wm. B. Eerdmans Publishing Co., gives greater detail.

7. "When a site has been occupied for many centuries, the remains from the successive periods of its occupation lie one above another 'in such a way as to suggest a gigantic layer cake.' Stratigraphic digging, which is the basis of modern scientific excavation, means digging in a manner that the superimposed occupational levels are kept distinct. The remains found in each layer, particularly pottery, must be exactly and meticulously recorded, so that comparative study with other similar levels in other sites will yield correct dating and accurate conclusions."
—Merrill F. Unger

8. Andre Parrot, *Abraham and His Times* (Philadelphia: Fortress Press, 1968), p.101. For some earlier indications see Joseph P. Free, "Abraham's Camels," *Journal of Near Eastern Studies,* July, 1944, pp. 187-193.

9. *Life,* December 25, 1964, p. 39.

10. *Ibid., op. cit.,* p. 10.

11. Quoted from *Lessons for Intermediates,* Lesson 3 for Nov. 23, 1947, in *Western Voice,* April 28, 1950, p.7.

12. *The Letters to the Seven Churches* (Grand Rapids: Baker Book House, reprinted 1963), p. 3.

13. *Our Bible and the Ancient Manuscripts* (New York: Harper and Brothers, 1941), p. 4

14. *Researches in Sinai* (New York: E.P. Dutton and Co., 1906), p. 132.

15. "Some Reasons Why," V. From Robert Ingersoll, *Lectures,* Vol. II (New York: Dresden Company, 1902), p. 291.

16. At Carthage "for the first time sufficient evidence accumulated to show conclusively that the ancient stories of Phoenician and Canaanite infant sacrifice to 'Molech' were only too true, and that the Jerusalem topheth which Josiah defiled while destroying idolatrous practices in Judah was indeed a place where a man 'might make his son or his daughter to pass through the fire to Molech.' It is now clear that other peoples' detestation of the Phoenicians for such a practice was founded on fact." Donald Harden, *The Phoenicians* (New York: Frederick A. Praeger, 1962), p. 95.

17. *Time,* December 13, 1963, p. 59A.

18. Rogers, Adams, Brown, *Story of Nations* (New York: Holt, Rinehart, and Winston, 1965), p. 59.

19. *Sunday Bulletin,* October 1, 1967, p. 25.

20. "The Bible as Divining Rod," *Horizon,* November, 1959, pp. 4-19, 118, 119.

21. *Horizon, op. cit.,* p. 118.

22. Yigael Yadin, *Masada* (New York: Random House, 1966), p. 54 picture caption. Picture on p. 55.

23. Glueck, of course, read from the Hebrew Bible, not the King James Version.

24. The Arabah is part of one of the great cracks of the earth. It extends from Lebanon to the Red Sea. The Jordan River flows down this valley. The great Rift Valley of East Africa is but an extension of it.

25. *The Other Side of Jordan* (New Haven: American Schools of

Oriental Research, 1940), p. 87.

26. *Ibid.*

27. "The Old Testament and Archaeology" in Alliman and Flack, *Old Testament Commentary* (Philadelphia: the Muhlenberg Press, 1949), p. 138. The Table of Nations is thoroughly discussed by Dr. Merrill F. Unger, *Archaeology and the Old Testament* (Grand Rapids: Zondervan Publishing House, 1954), chapters 6-8.

28. Glueck, *Horizon,* pp. 9-10.

29. *Other Side of Jordan,* p. 99.

30. "Phoenicia and the Ivory Trade," *Archaeology,* Vol. 9, No. 2 (Summer, 1956), p. 92.

31. See pictures in *National Geographic,* March, 1965, p. 420f.

32. *Horizon, op. cit.,* p. 118.

33. Symposium by the American Scientific Affiliation, p. vi. Now out of print.

34. Zeus, chief god of the Greek pantheon. The Greek philosophers who rejected polytheism elevated him to the position of supreme cosmic mind of the universe.

35. *Bibliotheca Sacra,* October, 1964. Reprinted in *Studies in the Bible and Science* (Grand Rapids: Baker Book House, 1966), Chap. XI. Dr. Morris is an engineer and scientist, a Christian who holds his master's and doctorate in Civil Engineering Hydraulics. He has written several books on aspects of the relationship between Scripture and science — all well worth reading.

36. *Seven Reasons Why A Scientist Believes in God* by A. Cressy Morrison (Old Tappan: Fleming H. Revell Co., 1962).

37. *The Twilight of Evolution* (Grand Rapids: Baker Book House, 1964). For the reply of a professional biologist to evolution, see Bolton Davidheiser, *Evolution and the Christian Faith* (Nutley, N.J.: The Presbyterian and Reformed Publishing Company, 1969).

38. Robert Dick Wilson would read "cease to shine" instead of "stand still"; see *Moody Monthly* (October, 1920). Thus producing extended darkness to cover the victorious Israelites. (See also Maunder, "The Battle of Beth Horan" in *International Standard*

Bible Encyclopedia). Another suggestion has been the refraction of the light of the sun, A. Randle Short, *Modern Discoveries and the Bible* (London: Inter Varsity Fellowship, 1947), p. 116f. Harry Ironside, in his *Addresses on the Book of Joshua* (Neptune, N.J.: Loizeaux Brothers, 1966) p. 103f quotes scientists who suggest that a day was lost in astronomical reckoning.

39. *The Old Testament and Archaeology,* from Old Testament Commentary, edited by Herbert C. Allerman and Elmer E.F. Flack (Philadelphia: Muhlenberg Press, 1948).

40. Harry Rimmer, *That Lawsuit Against the Bible* (Grand Rapids: Eerdmans Publishing Company, 1956).

41. The nebular hypothesis is a Frenchman's theory to explain how our solar system was formed. According to this theory the sun and planets were formed from a nebula, or cloud, of intensely heated gas. Gravitation made the nebula condense to form globes.

42. Anthropomorphism — an interpretation of what is not human in terms of human characteristics. For example, to say that God has arms.

43. *Time,* July 4, 1955, pp. 42, 43.

44. For more detailed treatment of miracles as they attest to the revelation of God's Word, see Strong's *Systematic Theology,* pp. 117-133.

45. Brinton, Christopher and Wolff, *A History of Civilization,* Vol. I (Englewood Cliffs, N.J.: Prentice, Hall, Inc., 1958), p. 133.

46. Joseph Klausner, *From Jesus to Paul* (Boston: Beacon Press, 1943), p. 260.

47. *Miracles, Yesterday and Today* (Grand Rapids: Wm. B. Eerdmans Publishing Co., 1954), pp. 25-26.

48. II Chronicles 22:2 may be rendered "granddaughter of Omri." Compare with 21:6.

49. *Op. cit.*

50. *The Unity of Isaiah, a Study in Prophecy* (Philadelphia: Presbyterian and Reformed Publishing Co., 1950), p. 1.

51. *Ibid.*

52. *The Oxford Annotated Bible* (New York: Oxford University Press, 1965), p. 657.

53. D.D. Luckenbill, *Ancient Records of Assyria and Babylonia,* Vol. I (Chicago: University of Chicago Press, 1927), p. 304.

54. Robert W. Rogers, *Cuneiform Parallels to the Old Testament* (New York: Eaton and Mains, 1912), p. 382. Compare with Pritchard, *Ancient Near Eastern Texts* (Princeton University Press, 1950), p. 316.

55. *In and Around the Book of Daniel* (Grand Rapids: Zondervan Publishing House, 1963), p. 2. This is a reprint of a book first published in 1923.

56. William S. LaSor, *Amazing Dead Sea Scrolls and the Christian Faith,* Revised (Chicago: Moody Press, 1959), p. 44, quotes Driver, *The Hebrew Scrolls,* p. 935, and adds: "Driver has since accepted an early date for the DSS; I have not however seen any further statement by him relevant to the date of Daniel." It might be added that in his "Introduction to the Old Testament of the NEB," he still maintains a second-century date for the end of the Old Testament period, which certainly implies he still holds that late a date for Daniel.

57. Merrill F. Unger, *Archaeology and the Old Testament* (Grand Rapids: Zondervan Publishing House, 1954), p. 298.

58. A.T. Olmstead, *History of Assyria* (New York: Charles Scribner's Sons, 1923), p. 282.

59. A.T. Olmstead, *Persecution and Liberty* (Essays), n.d., p. 44.

60. Robert Dick Wilson, *A Scientific Investigation of the Old Testament* (Philadelphia: The Sunday School Times Co., 1926), pp. 81, 82.

61. *Ibid.,* pp. 84, 85.

62. *Darius the Mede, A Study in Historical Identification* (Grand Rapids: Wm. B. Eerdmans Publishing Co., 1959), p. 66.

63. Brinton, Christopher and Wolff, *Civilization in the West* (Englewood Cliffs, N.J.: Prentice-Hall, 1964), p. 68.

64. Merrill D. Peterson, *The Jefferson Image in the American Mind* (New York: Oxford University Press, 1962), pp. 300-304.

65. *The Bearing of Recent Discovery on the Trustworthiness of the New Testament* (Grand Rapids: Baker House, 1953), p. 38. (A Baker reprint).

66. Brinton, Christopher and Wolff, *Ibid.*, p. 67.

67. *Are the New Testament Documents Reliable?* (Grand Rapids: Wm. B. Eerdmans Publishing Co., 1954), p. 16.

68. *Ibid.*, p. 20.

69. *Eternity* (June, 1972), pp. 25-33.

70. *The Bible and Archaeology*, (New York: Harper and Brothers, 1949), p. 288f; quoted by Bruce, *op. cit.*, p. 24.

71. Frank Morison, *Who Moved the Stone?* the Evidence for the Resurrection (New York: Barnes and Noble, Inc., 1962).

72. *Time*, December 10, 1965, pp. 96-97.

73. E. M. Blaiklock, *The Archaeology of the New Testament* (Grand Rapids: Zondervan Publishing House, 1970), p. 78f.

74. *Miracles* (New York: The MacMillan Co., 1947), pp. 16-17.

75. "Lyttelton" *Lives of the Poets,* Vol. II of The World's Classics edition (London: Oxford University Press, 1942), p. 488.

76. *Collected Works of George, Lord Lyttelton* (London: J. Dodsley, 1774), pp. 269-331.

77. December 25, 1964. (Special double issue on the Bible).

78. *Op. cit.*, p. 310.

79. C. K. Barrett, *The New Testament Background:* Selected Documents (New York: Harper and Brothers, Torchbook edition, 1961), pp. 48-49.

80. "Extraordinary Diaries of Winston Churchill's Personal Doctor," *Life,* Vol. 60, No. 16 (April 22, 1966), p. 98.

81. *Op. cit.*, p. 488.

82. Sir William Ramsay, *The Bearing of Recent Discovery on the*

Trustworthiness of the New Testament, Chapter II (Grand Rapids: Baker Book House, 1953), pp. 7-31. This chapter is autobiographical.

83. Mrs. T. H. Worchester, *The Life of David Livingstone* (Chicago: Moody Press, 1888), p. 126.

84. H.A. Ironside, *Random Reminiscences* (Neptune, N.J.: Loizeaux Brothers, 1929), pp. 99-107.

Selected Bibliography

Blaiklock, E.M. *Out of the Earth.* Grand Rapids: Eerdmans
Publishing Co., 1957.
Companion book to J.A. Thompson's book mentioned below.
Covers New Testament. Quotes monuments extensively.
Recommended for easy reading.

Boyd, Robert T. *Tells, Tombs and Treasure.* New York: Bonanza
Books, 1969.
A pictorial guide to Biblical archaeology. Abundantly
illustrated and popularly presented material.

Bruce, F.F. *Are The New Testament Documents Reliable?* Grand
Rapids: Eerdmans Publishing Co., 1954.
A must for every Bible student's library. One of the standard
works.

Criswell, W. A. *Why I Preach That The Bible Is Literally True.*
Nashville: Broadman Press, 1969.
A great preacher's able defense of the basis of his ministry.

Glueck, Nelson. *The Other Side of the Jordan.* New Haven:
American Schools of Oriental Research, 1940.
A prominent Jewish scholar describes his experiences
excavating in the Holy Land by following Biblical clues.

Henry, Carl F. H., Editor. *Revelation and the Bible.* Grand Rapids:
Baker Book House, 1958.
A symposium by leading conservatives. Many of the chapters
are applicable to this book and each is written by a specialist
in the particular field.

Morison, Frank. *Who Moved the Stone?* New York: Barnes and
Noble, 1962.
Personal testimony of a lawyer forced by the evidence to
believe in a literal resurrection in spite of a liberal attitude
toward the Bible. He begins, "This is not the book I intended
to write . . ."

Morris, Henry. *Studies in the Bible and Science.* Grand Rapids:
Baker Book House, 1966.
A collection of the author's magazine articles. Highly
recommended.

Ramm, Bernard. *Protestant Christian Evidences.* Chicago: Moody Press, 1959.
Took first award in Moody Christian textbook competition.

Symposium, A. *Can I Trust My Bible?* Chicago: Moody Press, 1963.
Excellent collection papers written in popular style. Recommended to interested readers. Even an alert high school student can read these with pleasure and profit.

Thompson, J. A. *The Bible and Archaeology.* Grand Rapids: Eerdmans Publishing House, 1972.
Excellent book for popular reading with quotations from the monuments.

Unger, Merrill F. *Archaeology and the New Testament.* Grand Rapids: Zondervan, 1962.

Unger, Merrill F. *Archaeology and the Old Testament.* Grand Rapids: Zondervan, 1962.
Two up-to-date and comprehensive works. Dr. Unger is also a leading conservative scholar.

Unger, Merrill F. *Introductory Guide to the Old Testament.* Grand Rapids: Zondervan, 1951.
First prize winner Zondervan textbook contest.

Vos, Howard F. *An Introduction to Bible Archaeology.* Chicago: Moody Press, 1956.
A brief, non-technical explanation of the purposes, methods and results of Biblical archaeology.

Whitcomb, John C. Jr. *Darius the Mede.* Grand Rapids: Eerdmans Publishing Co., 1959.
Interesting study of an important problem.

Young, Edward J. *An Introduction to the Old Testament.* Grand Rapids: Eerdmans Publishing Co., 1949.
An important work by a leading conservative Old Testament scholar. Dr. Young teaches at Westminster Seminary.

Young, Edward J. *Thy Word Is Truth.* Grand Rapids: Eerdmans Publishing Co., 1957.
Wilbur Smith calls this the most important work on inspiration since Warfield.

Indexes

SUBJECT INDEX

INDEX OF SCRIPTURE REFERENCES